To Boldly Go

Eric Delve

To Sue,
Never forget that Jesus
loves you — rejoice!

[signature]

Sovereign World

Sovereign World Ltd
PO Box 777
Tonbridge
Kent TN11 9XT
England

Unless otherwise stated, all Bible quotations are taken from the
Revised Standard Version © Copyright 1946, 1952 by The Division
of Christian Education of the National Council of the Churches of
Christ in the United States of America.

GNB – Good News Bible © Copyright American Bible Society,
New York 1966, 1971, 1976.

NRSV – New Revised Standard Version © Oxford University Press
1989.

JBP – J.B. Phillips © William Collins & Sons, Glasgow.

AV – Authorised Version, Crown copyright.

NIV – The Holy Bible, New International Version © Copyright
1973, 1978, 1984 International Bible Society. Published by Hodder
& Stoughton.

ISBN 1 85240 103 6

Typeset by CRB (Drayton) Typesetting Services, Drayton, Norwich
Printed in England by Clays Ltd, St Ives plc.

Contents

This version of *To Boldly Go* is dedicated to my wife Pat, whose loyalty and love never cease. I have learned so much from her.

᙮   ᙮

I also owe an immense debt of gratitude to Bernie Garner who deciphered my writing and typed the manuscript, the leaders and congregation of St Lawrence, Kirkdale; and the Rhino Club whose members have become friends greater than brothers: Stewart Henderson, J. John, Mike Mitton, Russ Parker, Adrian Plass, Pat Lynch and Ian Petit.
Thank you all for being the means of grace.

Foreword

Often, people say in Forewords that you won't be able to put this book down. I want to encourage you to do the exact opposite. This book is layer upon layer of teaching, analysis, encouragement and advice. Don't just skim it, but read it carefully and thoroughly, a chapter at a time, taking space to work out the implications for your life. If you feel broken and scarred this book will help restore your spiritual health. You will find it like soothing ointment to your wounds.

Eric Delve holds nothing of himself back in this book. He weaves together his years of world-wide experience as an evangelist, his life and ministry as a pastor and his journey with Christ into the heart of God. His honesty and realism is breathtaking as again and again he shares himself; his successes, his failures, his insights and what is really on his heart. Each chapter speaks of the integrity of a man who journeys with God through the ups and downs of life, and has remained faithful because he has glimpsed the Kingdom of God.

The message comes through time after time: 'Live originally, not as a boring stereotype ... use your life wisely ... it matters what you do.' It is a call to urgent reassessment of our own lives and the corporate life of our churches, in the radical light of God. Not a God who is far off, who made creation and now watches passively by, but a God who upholds and sustains, a God who is intimately bound up in the life of His people, a God who has not left us in the dark, but has revealed Himself in the history of the world, the pinnacle of which is Christ. We can know God. We can know who God is. We can know that God has a plan for our lives. This is a wake-up call to Christians, to be aware of the kind of God who has saved us, to understand the implications of the world we are in, and the message of Jesus to that world.

Never in my lifetime has it been as important to grasp the issues at stake for us in the Christian life; 'unless we grasp the reality and vital importance of spiritual things we will live in the emptiness of materialism.' It is surely impossible for anyone to look around at the state of the world and be satisfied that things are as they should be. But this is not only true of the world; those of us who are Christians are painfully aware that we are not what we should be, and the same is true of our churches. This book meets us at exactly this point. But no reader will be left there.

Eric deals with many thorny issues which people ask me about all over the country, answering questions about our own personal calling and mission in life, our own fight against that because of our sin. He takes on apathy in the Church and calls us to have a huge vision of God, where God is constantly surprising us. There is a call to gutsy godliness and practical advice on what everyday holiness means. We see the vital place for a renewed commitment to the Bible and prayer in the reality of the spiritual battle which we are fighting. Before us is the final vision of reaching the heart of God, of experiencing the Kingdom of Heaven for eternity. As those in Christ we *can* know who we are, we *can* know what we are on earth to do; we only live once and we are responsible to live this life to the full for God. Yet we do not simply have hope for this life, for ahead of us lies the 'crown of glory'.

I commend this book to you highly. We are people with a glorious destiny living at a time when the only destiny the world is heading for is destruction. The call is going up around this country and the countries of the world; it is time to grasp the nettle, it is time to seize the day, not for ourselves but for Him who made us, who died for us, who rose and now reigns for us, and longs that we should be His people doing the work He set us apart to do before the creation of the world. Let us not allow this moment to pass us by. I hope and pray that reading this book you are able to 'press on to take hold of that which took hold of you.'

J. John

Prologue

The emergency session of the Inter-Galactic Council of the Heavens was nearly over. At its secret meeting place 'somewhere in the cosmos' debate had raged for a small eternity.

Finally the Archangel surveyed the assembly. 'We are all agreed then? There is only one man who can deal with this crisis – we must send for him.'

The decision was made. Momentous silence descended. The Archangel reached out; his hand hovered for a moment before coming down on the super-emergency call button.

Instantly the call raced across space and time until its silent clamour reached the ears of the Rev. Rock Firm, quiet-spoken, gentle minister of St Edburga-the-Less Church, Megalopolis. He stiffened for a moment and then rose from the table at which the Ladies' Bright Hour Committee were debating the annual outing to Brightsea.

'Please excuse me, Ladies,' he said. 'Duty calls me – an unexpected need.'

The ladies smiled – they were used to their dear minister and his rather absent-minded ways.

Outside the door of the room he was transformed. Dashing into his private vestry he shut the door. So fast that all movement was a blur, he peeled off his outer garments revealing a purple cape resting on powerful shoulders which were encased in a tight-fitting blue costume.

Powerful muscles rippled as his mighty thighs propelled him towards the window. Grabbing his special Super-Amplified Bible he launched himself upward from the window-sill.

A few blocks away some church members emerging from a prayer meeting looked up in amazement.

'Is it a bird?'

'Is it a plane?'

'No,' said a quiet voice, 'it's Superchristian.'

Ineffective, mild-mannered Christian sap Elmer J. Crud continued looking long after the purple missile had vanished from view. The others drifted home leaving him standing alone on the church steps. Sadly at last he turned to go, his shoulders drooping in despair, failure in his eyes! 'Oh gosh, Superchristian,' he whispered, 'I wish I could be like you.'

A Bit of History

Following the stupendous impact of the Harringay Crusade in 1954, Billy Graham almost decided to stay in Britain indefinitely. Musing on that possibility in 1963, David Frost wrote,

> 'What would have happened? Would we have become a nation as dull and narrow-minded as some of his followers? Or a nation as vibrantly alive and flagrantly Christian as Dr Graham himself? Or what? I wish he'd stayed.'

What a question! And how terrifying that it can be asked about a part of the body of the living Christ. The Church in the west still claims to proclaim the good news of Christ, who is the wisdom and dynamic of God; yet so many of us live lives that are 'dull' – colourless, characterless, featureless, pale and grey. How could the message of the living God in Christ produce a people so bland, so innocuous, so capable of being ignored, so boring?

There can be only one answer; an absence of Jesus Christ from our Christianity. Our only message is him and we cannot be God's messengers unless we are living the message.

I have often watched *Star Trek*. The opening phrases stick in my mind ...

> These are the voyages of the Starship Enterprise;
> Its five year mission;
> To explore strange new worlds;
> To seek out new life and new civilisation;
> To boldly go **where no man has gone before!**

Chapter 1

No Final Frontier!

The long search

We began the long search the moment we were born, some say even while in the womb. It was the quest for meaning, for significance, for love. What most of us take a long time to discover as we begin our voyage is that love is searching for us. Not the emotional lightning strike of being 'in love', nor the burning of physical desire, but the real thing. Love that is tireless, selfless, endless. The trouble is, we can find that kind of intensity worrying, unsettling. We start asking uneasily 'what do you want?' If that sort of love really lives in the universe we may find it frightening and discover ourselves edging towards the door – if only we could find it. It is one thing to search, quite another to be the object of someone else's search. In the end it is often easier to ignore it.

But if we do that, our need for relationship may ambush us or unexpectedly embarrass us. In an interview in the *Daily Telegraph*, August 31st 1992, Richard Dawkins, author of *The Selfish Gene*, explained his reasons for not believing in God to Mick Brown, who concludes his article with this quote:

> '"I've contemplated a tropical rainforest and felt a tremendous sense of awe, of worship ..."
> There is a pause. He didn't mean to say that.
> "Not, of course, that there is anything **to** worship."'

The Risen Christ is the key

His pronouncement is very much the voice of the western European at the edge of the 21st Century: apparently confident, the human race comes of age needing neither the company nor the help of any God; yet perhaps subconsciously uneasy. Strangely, it is not so far from the way many religious people live. A.W. Tozer, the prophetic analyst of modern Christianity wrote: 'Most Christians of my acquaintance live as pro-tem atheists.' He observed that most of us believing, 'Christ died for us' and 'Christ will come again' live in the present as if God were dead. Paul the apostle wrote that if Christ has not been raised, our faith can only give us a bit of spurious comfort in our brief lives and: *'we are of all people most to be pitied.'*[1] The old translation read *'we are of all men most miserable.'* It may not be a strictly accurate translation but it is still true. Without the fellowship of the risen Christ, Christianity can only disappoint us and make us miserable.

So many of us live like that: our vision of Jesus doctrinal and theoretical, not living and moving. Jesus, the one from heaven becomes like us, just another prisoner of our world. Prisoners in chains, we plod wearily our earthbound path and nothing raises our heads. But the heart of the Christian is the faith that Jesus is alive. He stands before us as the resurrection Christ, human and yet divine. As human he retains the scars and scale of his life in Roman Palestine. As divine, he is a colossus bestriding heaven and earth uniting the two in himself.

Somehow, through him heaven touches us and every moment of our lives is shot through with heavenly meaning. Through him earth in us is taken up into heavenly places and begins to be transformed. When our long search brings us at last to Jesus we discover that all along he was searching for us. Then in him we begin the most exciting journey ever – the journey into the heart of God.

Something must happen!

Christianity is not just a system of belief. It is a life to be lived to the full. Yet we can go on existing as if none of this were true. Agreeing to the doctrines of the resurrection and ascension, still we live as if he were really dead. We are people in limbo, not yet dead, not truly alive. Not sufficiently heavenly minded to be of any earthly use to God we cut no ice in this earth; not earthly minded enough to be of any heavenly use we find no real place in the outworking of heavenly strategy. We live in a spiritual desert where many of our number sicken and die and the others carry on drearily, trying to hide the dull ache of desperate emptiness. What are we to do? We know it should not be like this. There are moments; moments of spiritual longing when the ashen embers flare into life only to die down leaving us greater failures than we were before.

We know that the Archangel proclaimed, 'With God nothing is impossible.' Yet still apathy reigns. We record of our lives in him, 'Nothing happened', not seeing that this means we are no longer with God, for 'nothing' is impossible to him. 'Something' must happen where he is! He is the living God – to be with him is to live also.

There are many crises calling for our urgent attention but the most desperate need of the world is for the Church to stand up identifiably like Christ, having a character and quality that can only be explained by his resurrection life.

The Risen Christ lives in us
The purpose of the death of Jesus Christ was that his incarnation – his life in the flesh – should go on by the power of his risen life poured into the Church. We are meant to be like him. God has no rest homes for Christians who have accepted defeat as permanent, or who resign their commission on the grounds that life in heaven's army is too tough. He expects and has planned for our victory. So it must be possible, even if we have failed again and again, even if we have gone far away.

The good news is good news precisely because it says to the failure, 'You can make it.' Into the far country of despair and the valley of defeat comes the reality of gospel truth. God's government is 'at hand': so close you have only to stretch out a hand and take hold. There is a way out, a way up, a high way, a holy way, a guarded way. So why does it not work? Why do millions of Christians live in a constant state of spiritual defeat? They have tried – they have wished to be changed, only to be defeated again and again until dull resignation sets in: 'Guess I'll always be defeated.'

So what is wrong? What is the missing element? For many it is the total absence of any assurance that their lives mean anything – feeling that whatever happens to me, my small struggles, occasional victories and the defeats that devastate me are still of no real consequence. The great juggernaut of God's purpose rolls inexorably on – I don't matter, I don't mean anything. Modern philosophies rob us of true significance – all is relative. Our most terrible need is for a sense of personal value and a confidence in God who cares so much about each individual that he has carefully planned a destiny for **every** person.

Robbed of our true value

Like many ministers and evangelists, I have been faced with Christians who have said, 'I wish I could be like you.' They don't really know what they are saying. They might change their minds if they spoke to my family! People say this because they have no vision of their own destiny. They do not understand the truth of the gospel: 'The son of God loved **me** and gave himself for **me**.' So often we have been slow to realise that God made me to be me and not anybody else. He delights in the 'me-ness' of me, no matter how odd I may be. So Christian bookstalls dispose of ever mounting piles of biographies and autobiographies, because people who do not really know God, find something of reality in the experience of others who do know him. People who have never had a sense of their own meaning and destiny, never really had a purpose or direction, find it second-hand in the lives of others.

This vicarious excitement has limited usefulness; it provides evidence of the power of the living God. Power which can and does intervene in human lives and makes them utterly different. Yet it means that thousands of Christians never experience the real adventure of living with God. That is being enjoyed by somebody else. This in turn encourages a lessening sense of their own value, so they settle for being 'just an ordinary Christian'. Even worse, they may begin to believe in a pagan value system which means that clergymen, ordained ministers, evangelists etc., are automatically of higher value than people with other functions in the church.

I once received a letter from a man who said he was 'only a lavatory attendant'. The New Testament knows nothing of such judgements. The only hierarchy in heaven is the hierarchy of maturity in Christ. The real questions are: How well do you know God? How much you do love him? How deeply has his nature advanced into yours?

You are the only one
God has no 'special' people – some he uses in more obvious ways than others but all humans are special to him. He is a father and a mother; not a spiritual industrialist with an endless production line for turning out standard modules of spiritual life. His fatherhood and motherhood like his loving are infinite in their capacity. He knows your name, he named your family and has called you by name into his own family. God knows you and loves you. Neither is this love for you generalised. A girl once said to me in response to my saying 'God loves you', 'Well, he loves everybody doesn't he?' That is true but the perspective is wrong. It is not that God loves me because he loves the whole world. The truth is he loves the whole world because there is not a single human being in all of mankind's past, present or future who cannot say, 'God loves me, me, me.'

And that includes you. You are the precious, loved, desired child of a glorious, great, loving Father. And this relationship began long before you were born, in fact before the world or this universe was made. He loved you before ever he breathed the galaxies into being. However good or bad your earthly father may have been; however bad a child you may have been, God is your true Father for he fathered you in eternity long before all things were made.

And why you especially? Because you are you, a unique once-only expression of the living God made to hear, see and know him as no one else ever did, and then out of that knowledge to unveil before the watching world the revelation of God that only you can reveal. Since you are physically, biologically, intellectually, emotionally, psychologically never to be repeated; God will never have another chance in this universe to reveal the facet of his character that is uniquely for you to know and show. There will never be another one like you! Maybe your reaction is to say 'Thank God' – you would be right whatever your reason! This is one area where there are no mistakes – you are not an accident. Neither Satan's opposition nor man's rebellion has any effect on God's sovereign act of creation. He alone gives to each human that essential expression of his own life that is the soul, the spirit of a person. So you and I matter. We really do matter. But we must not allow this to become a heavy burden; or a matter of pride. Infinitely precious each of us may be, but we are each only a small part of the whole. It is when God puts us all together in the mystery that the Bible calls the body of Christ that the true glory is seen. Here in a fallen world the glory is revealed intermittently. One day the full glory of God will be seen in that body.

Why Satan hates you
Satan, of course, hates all this because he hates God. He has tried, does try and will try to ruin God's beautiful masterpiece. By crippling the body, genes and mind, breaking the heart, wrecking the psychology, he will try to prevent God's revelation into or out of the spirit of the human. He knows that by hurting you he can hurt God because he knows how important you are to God.

You see, your difference is part of the gospel, the good

news: God is a creator whose creative activity is endless – the Bible says the Father is constantly expressing himself by speaking out the Word. That Word is his only begotten son. We know him as Jesus. A word full of reason, intelligence, beauty, excitement, soaring imagination, design, personality, emotion, power. Through that Word all things exist. All things are little words coming from the one Word. Every person is, you are, another small word sprung from the one Word. God has got so much to say and you are part of it. His infinitely varied creative activity is constantly exploding with life – he is the living God.

But you do have a choice. He knows that nothing won by manipulation or force is any good to him, so when he made you he made an adventure and sent it out into creation to happen! But not carelessly. He has a plan which is the very best for your life and your adventure is to find that plan and live it. Jesus called this 'the good news of the kingdom of God'. This is the idea that here on this fallen earth an ordinary imperfect human may meet the living, eternal God, resign self-centred control and receive Jesus, the one Word, into himself or herself so that the whole of life begins to be an expression of God. It may be scary, very! But boring, never! They are living the kingdom of God, and God's splendour begins to stream out from them.

How many universes are there? However many there are in God's multi-dimensioned creation all of them are waiting for you – for you to be revealed as truly a son or daughter of God. It is for this that Paul says the whole creation is waiting, groaning with labour pains. So rejoice, be glad where you are at this moment. Thank God for making you a once-only creative act to make known his character in the world. And not in this world only but in the whole dimension of spiritual reality; the heavenlies.

This realm is the natural dwelling of the eternal God and all the archangels, angels, godly principalities and powers. This same God has fathered you in Christ so that all these beings may know more of him. Crazy as it may seem, the angels of God will never know him fully unless you become what you are finally meant to be; happy, holy and loving; an ordinary person filled with an extraordinary God – an irresistible combination.

Why Satan fears you

But there are also other inhabitants in this heavenly realm. Satan, the King of Emptiness, and all his deceiving spirits, fallen angels, demonic hordes. From his place in the heavenly dimension he reigns over the world's darkness, torment and despair. He claims this world for his own. Yet God has destined that he shall receive the final blow to his ruinous ambitions from the inhabitants of this planet. The whole rotten, stinking, evil, tottering edifice of Satan's kingdom will meet its final destruction at the hands of the church militant here on earth. The mortal wound he received at Calvary will be exploited by the Christians who proclaim it, and so accomplish his final defeat.

> *'So the huge dragon, the serpent of ancient times, who is called the Devil and Satan the deceiver of the whole world was hurled down upon the earth and his angels were hurled down with him. Then I heard a great voice in heaven cry: "Now the salvation and the power and the kingdom of our God and the authority of his Christ has come! For the accuser of our brethren has been thrown down from this place, where he stood before our God accusing them day and night. Now **they have conquered him** through the blood of the Lamb and through the word to which they bore witness. They did not cherish life even in the face of death!"'* [2]

What an amazing passage. Sometimes it is hard to believe it is the sober truth. We are to accomplish this victory of Christ's power over Satan. You have a part to play. We are told that Jesus will destroy the enemy by the brightness of his appearing and the breath of his mouth. That brightness is in you and the breath rests on you. You see you are a greater person than you knew!

Love is our security

When Jesus turned to the disciples and said, 'The Father loves you,' he was saying something enormous. The great Father-Creator is responsible for a universe which we know stretches out in all directions from this earth for a least 20,000 million light years. And he is instantly, fully always present in every part of it. Moving so fast that he is always everywhere, and therefore everywhere always at rest; he is the living God. This unimaginable greatness is summed up for us by Jesus as 'the Father'. But he was more definite, 'the Father **himself**'. In other words – the very core of his being, the essence, the centre, the heart of God. Contemplate it with wonder. Meditate quietly on it and rejoice. 'The Father himself loves you.'

How should we respond?

David's response in Psalm 18 was

> '*I love thee, O Lord, my strength. The Lord is my rock, and my fortress, and my deliverer, my God, my rock, in whom I take refuge, my shield, and the horn of my salvation, my stronghold.*'

Fierce love and driving certainty live in those lines. David was a man of action who had proved the total worth and dependability of the God of action. And the intimacy of his relationship is shown by the word 'thee'. When I was a child they told me this was the language of respect and of proper distance; the right servile tone for a poor human to use to the eternal God. But that is not the way we are to be. This is the language of closeness, of love. 'How do I love thee, let me count the ways' wrote Robert Browning to Elizabeth Barrett. Of course, we do not often now use 'thee' and 'thou' in our praying because it does not really fit modern speech. But it is worth remembering that the 'you' we talk to is close to us, closer than father, lover, friend, and different from the same 'you' known to our fellow Christians.

But we are not all Davids.

Your choices matter

Micah's world was like our own – wealth and corruption marched with oppression of the poor, and injustice, while orthodox religion provided a false cover for people who did not know God. So Micah appealed to individuals to stand out against the tide, stand up for their God and, above all, to know him.

> *'What is good has been explained to you, man;*
> *this is what the Lord asks of you:*
> *only this, to act justly,*
> *to love tenderly,*
> *and to walk humbly with your God.'*[3]

Your God, not someone else's God, but yours. No question in Micah's mind as to the God they were to know. The personal God of holiness, truth and gladness. He was the eternal One – the God of Abraham, Isaac and Jacob. Precisely because he was the God of those men, the same God, but not the same to them, he was the God each man of Israel was to seek and know. Any parent worth their salt knows that each child is fascinatingly different from the others and therefore is a slightly different parent to each one. Thank God! This is the way he is. He wants to lead us into real relationship, a love affair with the everlasting one not just for our sake but also for his delight.[4]

You matter

So you matter, you really do matter. The way you live makes a small but real difference to the out-working of the plans of almighty God. Put that way it certainly sounds crazy but it is the truth. Evangelists – and I am one – are always saying God has a purpose for your life. We need to apologise, because we have said it so often it has become a truism, a saying so common as to be boring. But this is the heart of the message of Jesus Christ. 'You can be what you are meant to be; by God's power, as you yield to his reign.' If you draw back then God's unfolding purpose for all things will be hindered or thwarted for a while. If you give him the government of your life, the kingdom of God will move onward in you. As a result you will become a beachhead of truth, peace, joy and love in a sordid world.

How to start? You can begin by believing and by committing that faith to the Father in a prayer, like this maybe:

> 'Father, my Father, I thank you that you love me and have always loved me.
> Thank you that you know why you made me.
> Thank you that I mean something in your plan.
> In weakness with all my failures, my good points and bad points I give myself to you.
> By your power freely given I will be what I am meant to be.
> Let your will be done in me.
> I trust you.
> Amen.'

Does it work? Can God take ordinary failures and make them heavenly success stories? What we want to do now is to look at some of the evidence.

Chapter 2

Mission Accomplished

'I have fought the good fight, I have finished the race, I have kept the faith. Henceforth there is laid up for me the crown of righteousness, which the Lord, the righteous judge, will award to me on that day.'[1]

Jesus – the true human

'The men in the church are so wet! Where are the real men?' The speaker was female, young and indignant. I had just spoken at the church Youth Fellowship and was staying with her parents. Since I had exulted in the manhood of Jesus and his power as a leader of men, she was entitled to ask the question. It is an issue we shall return to. What makes a real man? What has happened to our concept of manhood in the church? I suppose few children's hymns have been so influential as Charles Wesley's 'Gentle Jesus, meek and mild'. Language changes, and that famous first line has come to mean something quite different for many people today, possibly, 'Timid Jesus, weak and feeble'.

Such a concept has often dominated even church thinking. Thousands of children emerge from Sunday school careers with the impression that Jesus was an impossibly nice, rather effeminate man who was totally unrealistic about the world and unable to cope with its problems. They grow into adults who see him as the proverbial Innocent unwilling and unable to face the shadow side of humanity. Permanently insulated from all the world's nastiness by his own niceness, he finally succumbed to the bad men because he was too weak to do anything else. This caricature has too often taken up residence in the hearts of Christian men who have felt forced to choose between a spirituality built on a fake vision of Jesus and a macho manliness in which hatred and aggression are principal ingredients.

Jesus was a real man. The best and bravest there ever was, and in all the fiery trials he endured he was sustained by his knowledge of his destiny. Many of us know that his life fulfilled hundreds of prophecies and often, with the benefit of hindsight, it all looks cosily inevitable: God's programme of events running on schedule. But the gospels give us another picture; someone subject to temptations, assailed by sudden doubts and sometimes weary. Yet through it all he remained faithful to the Father because he was sure of God's purpose.

The child is father to the man
That assurance was real by the time he was twelve. The first visit to the Temple and participation in the Passover celebrations marked the beginning of his coming of age. Perhaps the trip from Nazareth to Jerusalem was the time chosen by Joseph and Mary to tell their son the amazing story of his marvellous birth. What did he think when he first saw the gleaming dome of the Temple, the great court of the Gentiles and Solomon's porch, knowing that the last time he had been there, as a baby, a holy old man now long dead had held him and thanked God, *'Now at last I can die in peace; for my eyes have seen God's salvation...'*?

The boy had obviously lived a quiet, normal life, although the family had lived for a while as refugees. From their behaviour it seems clear his parents had almost forgotten who he really was. The sudden sick realisation that he had not left Jerusalem with their friends and relations in the party heading back to Nazareth, made a mockery of the after-feast carnival atmosphere. They rushed back to the city to search in needless panic. When they finally found him, a country boy, from despised Nazareth in uncouth

Galilee, debating in cultured surroundings with university professors, their own guilt feelings and unease in such company showed clearly; 'Son, why have you treated us like this? How could you? Your father and I have been so worried looking everywhere for you.' His reply shows only a genuine puzzlement:

> *'Why did you have to look for me? Didn't you know that I have to be in my Father's house?'*[2]

Then he left with them to become a good carpenter and to await his Father's time. He was obedient to them: His humility was born out of his assurance of who he was. There was no need to assert himself, no need to rebel in order to find his identity. He had it and began to grow in it. He increased in respect with God and men. He must have been a good carpenter!

The man is always his Father's Son
Eighteen years go by and Jesus, now an adult, goes to see his cousin John in the wilderness. His sense of purpose shows as he persuades a reluctant Baptist to dip him as a sign of repentance for sin, when John knows and Jesus admits he has no sin of which to repent. *'It is right for us to do this to fulfil all righteousness,'* he says. Immediately the heavens open and he sees the Spirit of God descending like a dove and settling on him. He hears the voice of God's affirmation, *'This is my dear son, I am well pleased with him.'* At this moment he consciously joins battle with Satan in a war which will reach its climax at Calvary. Then out into the wilderness to be tested by Satan for almost six weeks. It is always the same; God does something and Satan reacts.

But it is the Spirit who leads him, drives him out to meet the enemy in the desert. Nearly six weeks go by in which the tempter hits him with every temptation known to the human race. But Satan is beaten, beaten by a man who is God's man with an absolute assurance that he is God's son.

27

At this moment of victory Satan tempts him to misuse his sonship to feed himself, then to deny it by accepting Satan's authority and lastly to presume on it by acting on a faith not founded in his Father's guidance.

Two of those temptations actually begin with *'If you are the Son of God...'* He attacks Jesus at the point of sonship. He knows if he can destroy Jesus' trust in God as Father he will make him as weak as any other human. Our insecurities so often provide Satan with opportunities for temptation. God has served notice in Christ; the battleground between heaven and hell is to be human nature. And in his own humanity, Jesus defeats Satan.

He returns to Galilee ablaze with power and authority. At the synagogue in his home town of Nazareth he reads these words from Isaiah:

> *'The Spirit of the Lord is upon me*
> *because he has anointed me*
> *to preach good news to the poor.*
> *He has sent me to proclaim release to the captives*
> *and recovering of sight to the blind,*
> *to set at liberty those who are oppressed,*
> *to proclaim the acceptable year of the Lord.'*[3]

Strangely stopping in mid sentence he omits, *'and the day of vengeance of our God'*. That awaits him at the cross.

The authority of the son and heir

Decisively closing the book he calmly declares that all these marvellous promises apply to him. In short, he is the Messiah. He challenges their cynicism, reminding them of Israel's long history of unbelief. In rage they all jump up, grab him and lead him to a nearby cliff-top in order to push him over. But *'passing through the middle of them he went away'*! Disappointing isn't it? A few thunderbolts at least, you might think. But you see, Jesus knew who he was and where he was to die. He also knew he had a lot to do before he died so he quietly slipped away. And he could do that because he was the one person there at ease; he alone was not screwed up with fear or tension, so it was simple to quietly, calmly walk away. Jesus' assurance of his destiny is something stamped upon every page of the gospels:

> *'I must preach the good news of the kingdom of God to other cities also; for I was sent for this purpose.'*[4]

> *'I do nothing on my own authority but speak thus as the Father taught me. And he who sent me is with me; he has not left me alone, for I always do what is pleasing to him.'*[5]

> *'Truly I say to you, the Son can do nothing of his own accord, but only what he sees the Father doing.'*[6]

These, however, are not the sayings of a person who lived under a heavy burden of rules and regulations, but of someone who moved constantly in a real relationship with the living God. This living God was daily guiding and instructing him; and Jesus delighted to obey him moment by moment; for the guidance and the obedience were born of love, evidence of someone who knew his life was of ultimate meaning. So in spite of the terrible strain of the spiritual warfare he was a happy person. As the psalmist says in Psalm 45 – more happiness was poured upon him than on any other human being.

The courage of the son
Above all, this sense of purpose held him as he contemplated the cross. He knew the world was in the control of the enemy – he called Satan *'the prince of this world'* – and he knew that he had come to rescue mankind by being the ransom paid to the cosmic gangster.[7]

> *'And what shall I say? "Father save me from this hour?" No, for this purpose I have come to this hour.'*[8]

John tells us that at The Last Supper the knowledge of his coming death filled Jesus with endless love for his disciples. So, in spite of their bitter quarrelling and proud refusal to wash each other's feet, he stripped himself, wrapped a towel round him and proceeded to wash their filthy feet himself. This humility was rooted in his certainty that God had given the whole universe into his hands.[9]

In the garden over the Kidron valley the air was heavy and still. Jesus prayed and John himself struggled to stay awake. The holy Lord of life, facing hell, sweated drops of blood. Suddenly the silence was destroyed by the clash of armour, and the dark night torn by military torches. John says Jesus walked forward to meet them *'knowing all that was to happen.'*[10] The purpose held him – the one who had set his face to go to Jerusalem because that was the only place for a prophet to die, was saying with body, mind and spirit, *'Not my will, but your will be done.'* What a man! And the courage it gave was enough. *'Jesus, knowing that all was now finished, said, "I thirst".'*[11] He knew what was happening and that carried him through to triumph; the triumph of the great cry, *'It is finished!'* Victory was his.

Jesus' sense of destiny is so obvious. His whole life was consciously the outworking of God's purpose – and for most of that life he was a carpenter. Jesus was a working man and that was his destiny – to live out God's sonship as a manual worker.

We are his brothers and sisters
That is also the destiny of the church; to live out God's purpose so that simply in being who we are, we praise him. Thank God the vast majority of Christians are not preachers, ministers, evangelists, and even those who are must live out their faith. Your function in the church is a minor matter, your calling is to be the person – the child of God – that the Father intended from the beginning.

Now if the eternal son of God needed a real sense of God's purpose and meaning for him, we obviously need such a sense much more. Jesus was the new Adam – the new model for human beings. He was the way we are all meant to be. His destiny was clearly stated in Old Testament prophecy because of his special function, for he is the beginner of a new kind of creation. We share his nature. We actually have the same origin so that Jesus unashamedly calls us his brothers. As he lived so we should live in this world – we **must** believe that God has a purpose and meaning for each of us. Just because it is not written down, it is not less real than Christ's, for it is written in God's heart and Jesus carries it in his strong hands. As he spreads those hands before heaven, all the heavenly beings in time and eternity know that God has intended something for us and they watch eagerly to see – will it happen?

The plodder who won
It has already happened for some people . . .

'Second-hand Shoes and Boots' the sign over the door read. Inside the workman's cottage a cheerful little man with a bald head was leading a Bible study in between boot mending. He was twenty-eight years old and by no means an exciting or dynamic character. In fact, nothing further from the Hollywood image of 'man of destiny' could be imagined. The most exciting thing he ever said of himself was, 'I can plod. I can persevere in any definite pursuit. To this I owe everything.' Yet this plodding little man on 31 May, 1792, preached a sermon which changed the history of the world. Its theme was the need for a missionary society and was summed up:

> Expect great things from God.
> Attempt great things for God.

The people who heard it were going home after the service when he grabbed the arm of another minister and asked in desperation. 'And are you after all, again going to do nothing?' Four months later the Baptist Missionary Society was formed – the beginning of the modern missionary movement. And the man responsible, William Carey, said, 'Few people know what may be done till they try and persevere in what they undertake.' At the end of his life he said, 'If God used me no one need despair.'

The persecutor who wept
That sounds very much like something written hundreds of years before by another bald-headed little man, who was bandy legged as well! But very different in character. Ambitious, cruel, greedy for money and power, the name Saul of Tarsus rang terror in the ears of the early church like the name of Himmler to the Jews of Europe in the 1930s. Jesus met this vicious little man and transformed him into a man who wept over the sins of others and felt deep pain when converts fell away from Christ. As Paul the apostle he was to say, 'I was the worst of sinners because I persecuted the body of Christ but God had mercy on me so that in the future even the worst sinners will realise God can save and use anybody!' What held this man to his course? 'God set me apart from birth.' He knew that entering the kingdom of God's son he had entered upon God's purpose for his life.

The skinny missionary
The Victorians were a people especially given to making heroes and few of them would have realised how similar the psychology of the famous apostle was to that of a skinny little Yorkshireman called James Hudson Taylor. A deeply sensitive, intense character in a frail body; given to bouts of deep melancholy, he was hardly in the wide screen hero mould. But he knew God wanted China to hear the gospel. Barnsley may not sound the most likely starting point for a world-shattering strategy, but that tough town never had a greater son. 'God give me China,' he prayed, and God heard him. 'I sometimes think that God must have been looking for someone small enough and weak enough for him to use, so that all the glory might be his, and that he found me.' Earlier in his life, this man who revolutionised missionary work said 'a deep consciousness that I was no

longer my own took possession of me.' He knew he was special, chosen.

The big fisherman

It took quite a time before that big-hearted, generous, quick-tempered man Simon Bar Jonah understood the same thing. Physically big and outwardly confident he was deeply flawed by insecurity and guilt and felt no confidence in his ability to serve God. Three times he was called before he finally capitulated to the claims of Christ on the quayside by Galilee. How often people have said, like him, 'Go away Lord, I am just not good enough.' And the reply comes as it did then, 'Enter my kingdom and you enter the realm of my choosing, not of yours. I have chosen you to bear fruit. I will make you a fisher of men.'

There is not the space to talk of more than a fraction, but these men found that becoming Christians released them into a specially chosen pathway, that fitted their feet and theirs only, and the further in it they walked the more clear the face of God became. The call that each received was special but not unusual, not something reserved only for the privileged few. It was special to them. And God has preserved the record of their individual calls because he wants us to understand that these stories are typical of the way he deals with all human beings including us. Totally down to earth, practical; such people have an assurance of their place in God's scheme, an overriding sense of his purpose in everything. Their lives have heavenly meaning. And other people recognise in their refusal to bow the knee to worldly values, satanic pressure or fleshly indulgence, that they have been with Jesus. Nobody ever accused such people of not being real men or women!

The muddy Mystic

What about the women, God's radiant women? St Teresa of Avila moving a baggage train from one convent to another was crossing a flooded river when the cart encountered a pot-hole. It crashed into the water. Pulling herself to the bank through muddy water while her possessions were carried downstream she was heard to say, 'Lord I do not wonder that you have so few friends when you treat the ones you have so badly.' Yet she endured this and much opposition to keep the flame of faith alive in a decadent church.

Joy under the Jackboot

Corrie Ten Boom endured the hell of Ravensbruck concentration camp sustained by the purpose, 'I must tell the world that there is no pit so deep that he is not deeper still.' Basilea Schlink, listening night after night as American and British bombers pounded her beloved Germany, prayed that Germany would lose the war! She knew that God would judge the regime that persecuted Jews and strangers and felt its guilt so deeply she could pray for defeat!

Mother of hundreds

Amy Carmichael, beautiful, well-to-do, single, known as 'Madcap' because of her high spirits and sense of humour, called Amma, 'mother' by the Tamils, rescued hundreds of girls and boys from service as prostitutes in Hindu temples. She wrote,

> 'Let me not sink to be a clod
> Make my thy fuel, flame of God.'

Her poems and writings inspired hundreds of men and women to become missionaries too. No wonder General Booth said, 'Some of my best men are women!'

One remarkable woman was responsible for giving the world a truly historic man, yet there was a terrible moment when it looked as though he would never live to be six years old. Susannah Wesley must have suffered agonies the night the rectory in which she lived caught fire. They thought all eight children were out, but then as the fire raged through the timber building the face of little five year-old John appeared at an upstairs window. Two men made a human

34

ladder and dragged him out seconds before the roof caved in! More and more, John Wesley realised he had been delivered for a purpose; he always said he was 'a brand plucked from the burning.' This driving sense of divine purpose never left him, and sustained by it he made the world his parish.

The unknown celebrities

These are names whose stories we know, but have you ever wondered just why God left us those long genealogies or why large parts of the Old Testament are occupied by lists of names? God knows these names mean nothing to us and that even the most saintly Christian would be hard put to get much inspiration from them, where the names are not married to a known story. But that is the whole point. We do not know their stories. God does. To him the names and the stories are known, loved and precious. These anonymous lists proclaim to us, 'God knows, God cares, **all** are special to him.'

Jesus said, *'A good shepherd calls his sheep by name.'* Each of us is called by name. Designed by the creator God for some purpose which is ours and ours only, when we convert to Christ we step out of death into life. Out of chaos into order. Out of nowhere into somewhere. Love makes a nobody into somebody. We become special.

I remember a beautiful young Chinese girl the night she finally committed everything to Jesus Christ in a university mission meeting. She beamed, she was radiant. 'I feel special, I feel special and I feel proud.' Exactly. This was not the vicious puffed-up pride which is hell's imitation. This was the real thing. Pride of family. Pride of belonging to the family of God; the sheer exulting privilege of being a member of Christ.

The fat Hero

What about our response to this? Perhaps D.L. Moody can help. A successful businessman and rising preacher, he was dissatisfied with the standard of his life. He knew God had

35

a purpose for him but he could not, would not, let God take charge. In Dublin for a Christian conference, he attended an all-night prayer meeting. The next morning Varley, who had prayed with him through the night, said, 'Moody, the world has yet to see what God will do with a man fully consecrated to him.' Moody pondered and analysed the words for weeks. '"The world has yet to see what God can do with and for and through a man who is fully and wholly consecrated to him" ... a man. Varley meant **any** man. Varley did not say he had to be educated or brilliant or anything else. Just a **man**. Well, by the Holy Spirit in me, I'll be that man.'

He weighed 300 pounds, had a face half covered by a bushy beard, spoke in a high-pitched nasal twang, and to the end of his life could not spell. But Dwight L. Moody became the greatest evangelist the world had ever seen. Man or woman, I give you his words to make your own.

Of course, some of God's people faced with his destiny have failed it and shown its value by losing it. Does it really matter? It is to the stories of some of them that we turn next.

Before we do you may like to meditate on this prayer.

> 'Oh God, I look at the apostles and the saints.
> I see that you ask, not for our perfection
> But our availability to work in us your miracles.
> I offer to you all my gifts and talents,
> All the resources of my personality.
> Take them and fulfil your purpose for my life,
> Through Jesus who finished his task.
> Amen.'

Chapter 3

Mission Aborted

'To every man somewhere in his lifetime, there comes a special moment, when he is figuratively tapped on the shoulder and offered a chance to do a very special thing, unique to him and fitted to his talents. What if that moment finds him unprepared, unqualified for the work which could be his finest hour?'

(Attributed to Sir Winston Churchill)

The Rivals

The baby was hairy. Really hairy! Not just covered by soft downy hairs but by red hair that looked like a hair-cloak. He had only just beaten his twin brother into the world, in fact that one, the smooth one, came in hanging on to 'hairy's' heel.

As she looked at them Rebekah sighed, not only with relief. Such competition even in the act of birth did not bode well for the future. In fact, the pregnancy had been a difficult one, at times as if a wrestling bout were going on inside her. For months she had endured the pain and discomfort until finally it had all been too much. Looking back later it was like a dream, but then it had been frighteningly real. Weeping, weary, at the end of her tether, she had known the darkness of depression, had wanted to die. But God had explained: The two babies in her womb were to father two nations which would be rivals but eventually the nation of the younger child would win and the nation of the older twin would serve the other.

The hairy hunk ...

The contrast in physical appearance was matched by a complete contrast of temperament. The firstborn was called Esau – it meant covering and in their language sounded like 'hairy'. What else could they call him? Esau grew fast. From the beginning he was skilful at everything physical. Hard, tough and fast, he was a natural athlete. With fast mood changes, a sense of humour and an impatience for anything that could not be settled quickly, obviously and preferably by physical means, he was clearly a leader of men. The easy confidence that comes with early physical prowess was always his, and he was a good hunter in a day when hunting was a real man's major task. No matter how fast the wild deer, Esau usually managed to kill one. Isaac, his father, was well pleased: Such a son would make a worthy leader of the growing clan, and in the meantime ... Of course, it was true that Esau seemed to have no real sense of God, but he was young. He had plenty of time to learn all that.

Isaac had been forty before he married, and sixty when the boys were born. Though he had long known that his father's God was real, he had never really known God in the same way. Indeed it had not seemed necessary. Abraham had lived on into Isaac's own old age – the fierce faith in God that had sustained his long life had burned bright; bright enough for the whole family right to the end. The boys were fifteen when he died and well schooled in the history of the covenant; the Holy Agreement that Abraham had made with the only One, the living God, that his family would serve that living God alone. And there was the Promise. This God, the Maker, grieving over humanity's wickedness had promised that through Abraham and his heirs the whole world, every tribe and nation, would receive blessing. Esau had listened dutifully enough but his spirit chafed, longing to be back in the hunting grounds. Then again, the restrictions of the Agreement seemed unreasonable. Why should it be frowned upon to marry outside the family of the covenant? If a person was in love, surely that was enough.

... and the fast-talking smoothie

Jacob they had named the other boy – 'the grabber' – and
he, on the other hand, listened greedily. Let Esau have his
juvenile pursuits – he did not know what mattered, Jacob
did. Jacob knew the most precious thing the family pos-
sessed was the Agreement with Promise – the covenant.
And he wanted it. After all, he was nearly as old as Esau
and but for an accident of order would have been first-born
anyway. The first-born's birthright was a double share of
the property, and to be steward of the covenant. The property he didn't really care about. He wanted the covenant.
Daily he brooded on it as he stayed at home in the tents
helping with the cooking – smooth Jacob, a figure of fun to
many who saw him as the hairless wonder beside his macho
brother. Strangely, it was the cooking which gave him the
key – it was a good thick stew full of vegetables, flavoured
with lentils, savoury and coloured by red spices. The almost
smokeless fire of animal dung had brought it to perfection;
it simmered gently, little bubbles breaking on the surface
and releasing appetising fragrance into the air.

That day had been a bad one for the hunters. Most
unusual of all, even Esau had failed to find a deer; there
was to be no venison roasting over the fire this evening.
Disappointment nagged. An empty stomach is hard for an
impatient person to bear. As they came back to the camp
the mouth-watering aroma of Jacob's cooking drew Esau as
surely the perfume of the pitcher plant draws flies into its
lethal trap. He looked at his brother, they did not always
see eye to eye but surely ... a bowl of stew.

'That looks good, really tasty.'

'It is.' Jacob quiet, always watchful, said no more than
was necessary.

'I'm starving, give me some of that red stew.'

Typical Esau, a day out hunting and he was always starving.

'Sell you some if you like; for your rights as the first-
born.'

Jacob tried to sound casual but there was an edge, a

39

hardness in his voice that betrayed him. Esau eyed him strangely – he had always known that Jacob wanted his position. In fact the whole thing was a nuisance. He had never wanted the responsibility. Slightly angry, he agreed.

'All right. I am starving to death. What good will my rights do me if I die?'

'Swear it before God – the first-born rights are mine.'

And Esau swore a vow giving his rights to Jacob.

The terrible choice

But there was time for him to grow, maybe to change. Seasons passed and the young men matured. Esau at forty was entering his best years. So he decided to marry. He chose two Hittite women who were forbidden by the terms of God's Covenant. It was the seal on the bargain he had made years before with Jacob. That had been the act of an immature and fiery young man. In the heat of the moment he had said 'What I want **now** matters more than some future promise of God.' Choosing these women just because he wanted to, demonstrated that his attitude remained the same. God accepted the bargain.

Isaac, now blind, thought he was dying. Jacob took advantage of his blindness to cheat Esau out of the vital deathbed blessing, the passing of the blessing of God from the head of the family to the next head of family. It was now that Esau realised what he had thrown away and desperately tried to regain his destiny. The line of God's Messiah was his privilege but he had thrown it away, first for a bowl of stew, later for two pagan women. As the realisation hit him that his life would mean nothing, the tough hunter broke down and wept, begging for a position from which he could change his decision but he could find nowhere. God's destiny now rested firmly on Jacob, though he had yet to learn that God is not manipulated by human scheming, but responds to the deepest desires of men's hearts.

The terrible anguish of Esau echoed down the years, and though he eventually forgave Jacob he could never forget what he had lost. He had not lost his salvation. Indeed

Jacob was later to say his face was like the face of God. He had thrown away God's purpose. That purpose passed to Jacob's family and the prediction that Esau's nation would be slaves to Jacob's nation was fulfilled. Over thirteen hundred years later God said through Malachi, '*Jacob* (the nation) *I loved and Esau* (the nation) *I hated.*' For after Esau died his nation became implacable enemies of Israel and of God's plans.

The eternal seems unreal

Esau's problem was that the eternal purpose of God was unreal compared to what he could see, touch, feel, taste and hear. Pampering his flesh meant more than heavenly reality. Because he had no sense of destiny he was powerless to resist the temptation to immorality and indulgence. And many of us today are in his position. Although we believe the right things we live as materialists.

And our outlook becomes increasingly materialistic. The great problem is that selfish exploitation of things leads us to see people more as resources to be exploited, things to be used:

'Planned obsolescence' has been disastrous for the environment and the long-term economy of the earth. The problem is that its philosophy is written more and more into our relationships. Rich self-indulgent societies always become sexually immoral societies. The pleasures of sin **are** pleasurable – for a while. But the fun does not last long. Fear of Aids or resurgent sexually transmitted diseases, regret and guilt all combine to rob our pleasures of any real sense of fun. And the growing sense of disillusion, of emptiness, has a nasty habit of reaching back to steal from us even the good times in the past.

We have to learn not to treat ourselves as if we are lumps of meat without any ultimate meaning. We are humans made in God's image. Our bodies are not just mechanisms for short term enjoyment. We must not fall for the lie of the Devil. God has promised to crown us with his kingdom and glory. That is our destiny. And repentance is the way in.

There is a way back

A horse exercise ring on Epsom Downs may seem a strange place to find someone praying at three o'clock in the morning, especially a person who has deliberately sought out an area of horse dung in which to kneel. I looked for that place because it seemed to me to fit my spiritually filthy state. As I knelt in the dirt I remembered my Christian home, my calling to Christian service and the fatal rebellion against God's daily reign. Running from God I was out of control and soon totally dominated by my sexual drive, my false god. Still I had held the tattered shreds of a religious faith around me, a form of godliness without power. Sliding away from God, immorality, a time of repentance and cleansing, then quite deliberately the act of sexual rebellion which had brought the understanding of my defilement. The tears came.

'Lord, have mercy, I am a sinner. I do repent.'

'My son, what do you want?'

'To be clean, to live in purity.'

'Do you really? If you want the life of fleshly indulgence that is your choice.'

'I want you. I want your will.'

But it was just a little too routine. Even I could not tell whether my tears were genuine or produced in order to convince God and myself of my true sorrow and repentance. I had an uncomfortable feeling that they were induced for effect.

Suddenly, almost as if spoken by an audible voice I heard 'Esau sold his birthright for a pot of stew and afterwards could find no place to repent though he sought it with tears.'

I knew I was being told, 'This is your last chance. Once more like tonight and you will have made Esau's choice. You can be an Esau if you want.' The last sentence hung in the air.

At that moment I knew that a person who possesses everything but God, has nothing. Christianity is not just: 'Jesus died for you', but the reign of God advancing ever deeper into each human life.

Two roads lie within us

In the middle of me there is a great empty hole – a longing to be loved, to be approved, to matter. When I have responded badly to that void the result has been evil. When I have responded in a good way the result has been good. The roads to hell and to heaven lie within us.

On those occasions when I have made peace with God and allowed him to fill the emptiness, the ache has died, peace has come and I have been liberated. I have been free to serve others in a way that comes from love. Then comes the flow of appreciation from people that is so joyous and rewarding and dangerous. For it can seduce my soul from its rest, inducing it back to the treadmill.

I am familiar with the treadmill. When I approach others for my emptiness to be filled, however subtly I do it, this tends to isolate me from them. Like anyone in ministry I can use that ministry to generate appreciation from others. But when I minister **for that purpose** the satisfaction is always temporary. The longing is satisfied for a moment. Then I am back to the treadmill.

Only God can give me rest. Only his approval fills up the void.

I responded to the voice: 'Lord, I turn from my sin. I will never walk that way again. From now on, you are my King – I will obey you.' Today it is my greatest joy to tell people, 'Jesus gives you victory over sin,' for I have proved it, not without temptation, not without stumbling, falling and tears. But God has liberated me, given me rest, and has set me on the road to holiness. Not that I think I have arrived! Oh no. But on the evidence, I trust **him** to get me there.

Our God is so good! He rescues us even from our own stupidity when we call upon him. Nobody ever demonstrated that more clearly than the son of Manoah, yet his life was one of the great tragedies of Israel's story.

The mighty man who failed

The people had entered the promised land of God's gift only to rebel against him and lose his protection. The cruel hordes of the Philistines reigned over the land. They ravaged the countryside taking anything of value or beauty and gave the glory to their demonic false gods. God's name was dragged through the dust of Israel's despair.

Then the Lord acted, sending an angel to a childless woman whose husband was called Manoah. As is so often the case, Manoah was spiritually sleepy while his wife was awake to God, and obedient to his moving. In this case the messenger was a special one, 'the angel of the Lord', whom many believe to have been the son of God before his incarnation as Jesus Christ. The angel appeared twice to the woman telling her she would have a male child who would belong to God from the moment of his birth. Manoah did not believe the messenger was from God and tried to put him to the test by appealing to his vanity. The angel leapt into an altar fire and ascended in the flame. Then Manoah finally got it! It was really God. In due time his wife gave birth to a boy whom they named Samson. But a strong man needs a strong and godly father if he is to be a truly holy man. And Manoah did not know God well enough.

Samson grew. God's spirit began to stir in him. He was a deliverer to Israel. He destroyed Philistine crops, slew a lion with his bare hands, decimated whole armies sent against him, and once lifted the Gaza city gates with their posts and lintel on to his shoulders and set them up on the top of a hill. He was incredible. For twenty years the Israelis sheltered behind his enormous God-given strength. But his upbringing had left him dangerously deficient. He never truly understood that his strength was given for God's purpose and that it should be allied with moral purity. He only knew it had something to do with his hair being sacred to God so never cut it. When eventually this secret was prised from him, it was his undisciplined sex life that had betrayed him, long before Delilah had.

Few pictures are so pathetic as that of the shorn lion, poor Samson, his hair cut off, thinking he still had his supernatural strength: *'He did not know that the Lord had left him.'*

God can transform our failure

The Philistines took him, gouged out his eyes and chained him at the mill-wheel in the prison. Poor stupid Samson, caught by a woman he loved, ridiculed by the people who for so long had lived in fear of him. What could be more hopeless? The God he had betrayed seemed to have abandoned him. But. (Marvellous word 'but',) God was at work in Samson and his hair began to grow again. Even when we fail, God's love goes on. The Philistines sent for Samson to make fun of him at the great feast of thanksgiving to their cruel god Dagon. But they did not know who was coming. God was renewing Samson.

Listen to his last prayer:

> *'O Lord God, remember me, I pray thee, and strengthen me, I pray thee, only this once, O God, that I may be avenged upon the Philistines for one of my two eyes.'*[1]

And God heard – he could not change the past, could not give Samson back what he had lost, but Samson was giving God the mess he had made and saying, 'God use it if you can.'

The answer came, 'I can and I will.'

The strength of heaven flooded into him. He gripped the two centre pillars of the temple of Dagon and listened to the jeers of the enemies of God's people. Never again would they laugh at Samson, or his God.

'Let me die with the Philistines.'

Then he bowed those mighty shoulders for the last time and full power poured through the muscles. The pillars collapsed under the assault and the roof caved in on all the Philistine leaders and people that were there. He killed more enemies in his death than in all his life. What a man. But what a tragedy that he only became what he should have been at the very end. However even in his failure he points the way forward in history to Jesus whose greatest victory was achieved in apparent failure and death.

Still the same old story

God save us from repeating his story, yet it happens. I visited a college to speak to a Christian Union. The president spoke to me after the meeting, in some distress, about her concern for the membership. Out of fifteen members three were sleeping regularly with boy/girl friends. In fact, two members were more or less living together in a hall of residence. The really terrible thing is that none of the people concerned could be persuaded that this was not right.

They were totally unrepentant. In the 1970s at least one in every twelve young people in our churches had or were having intercourse outside marriage. Today no one would doubt the proportion is nearer one in two. People are at risk of throwing away their destiny. Sexual immorality may infect them with more than Aids. They may go so far down the road of rebellion as to make it difficult for God ever to use them. Even when they have repented, it may be impossible to restore to them their life's work. Don't let anyone deceive you, you cannot play games with God. Whatever you put into life you will eventually get back.

Unless we grasp the reality and vital importance of spiritual things we will live in the emptiness of materialism. Sometimes, aching, we will grasp at the flesh around us for our consolation. At other times we will grab at money and things. Especially as we grow older. For 'things' are so reliable. Even when we are spiritually and morally dead, emotionally exhausted and physically debauched things still whisper or shout, 'Here I am, solid, mechanical, offering guaranteed repeatable experience.' But how stupid to live for a video recorder. A lady I know once said to me, 'We bought the biggest and best TV Eric. It's worth spending out on one when you get to our age. After all it's our life now.' Maybe the biggest obscenity of our age is the extent to which the lives of people in the Western world, even Christians, are dominated by the acquisition of things, and the consumption of needless food.

The King who was a fool

The story of King Saul is a warning to us today. He was a herdsman before God made him king. The point of rebellion for him was the moment when he should have destroyed the Amalekite cattle and sheep. He killed the soldiers of the Amalekite army but the herdsman in him would not let him kill cattle. He was called to be king, a warrior in a battle, which had spiritual meaning, but he reverted to the values of his old life. Not for him God's 'well done' or the security of knowing he was doing God's will, he wanted to be able to count his security materially. In order to be God's king he had to turn from his old nature but it was the herdsman he obeyed. We all carry two natures within us. The quality of our lives will be governed by our response to them. Saul refused to let God's purpose, God's destiny for him, be his only guide. He died in despair falling on his own sword and his epitaph he had spoken himself: 'I have been a fool. I have gone sadly wrong.' Yet he never really repented. Unlike Samson the end is un- relieved gloom.

Pride sits so easily with materialism. Perhaps that is because things serve our selfishness, without involving us in even the residue of relationship. Material things are so seductive, enabling us to arrange our surroundings so that we are comfortable, always affirming to us that we are important. Perhaps that is why we get so angry when the car just will not start? After years of living in such a way we may like Saul, have become thoroughly infected by pride but still be religious. Indeed, we may well be a minister, a church officer, a deacon, an elder, a member of the PCC. Pride is a respectable sin, often surfacing in church relation- ships, turning the gateway to heaven into something like an anteroom of hell. At such moments Jesus must weep over his Church.

The frightening thing about this is that although we may not be serving God at all, we may still **think** we are. Such service will not last five seconds in the radiance of the holy God. He is a consuming fire. All that is placed before him is tried by that fire. The outshining of his purity, love and truth will burn up all that is not made by him.[2]

The commitment we must make
May God grant to you and me the power of his Holy Spirit so that our service may endure the radiation of his holiness, being made of heavenly materials. Otherwise we shall know the pain of the one who is saved *'through the flames'*. This must come very close to what Revelation calls *'hurt by the second death'*. The promise is that if we will commit ourselves to the Lord through all suffering, persecution and pain, we shall not be hurt by the second death. For all that is selfish and hellbound in us will already have been purged out by his indwelling.

We must have a sense of our special destiny or we shall not find the strength to fight sexual lust, the love of things and pride; and we shall end up being castaways.

Will you, just now, take a few moments to survey the areas of life we have looked at, then claim the cleansing power of the death of Jesus?

> 'Lord by your death clean me from lusts of the flesh, the love of things and pride. Liberate me from their power. Reign in me. Wake me up. Above all, do not allow me to become useless. I will not serve any other master. Jesus Christ is Lord. Amen.'

We have looked at some negative pictures – so many people have got it wrong and are doing so today. How do we get it right? It's the 'how' we now want to look at.

Chapter 4
Darkness Roaring – Daystar Rising

'Now this is not the end. It is not even the beginning of the end. But it is perhaps the end of the beginning.'[1]

Human beings – image and likeness of God

In the beginning ... God created. And he did that because he is creator – it is part of his character. He has always been and always will be engaged in a constant unfolding of creative activity. Because he is the living God. There is nothing static, dead or boring about him!

So if his people are static, dead and boring it is because they have ceased to reflect his nature. The very name 'Yahweh' given to Moses as God's name thousands of years ago bears this out. Though usually translated as 'I am what I am', its meaning becomes clearer as 'I am becoming what I am becoming'. This living God is limitless, and is constantly revealing more of what he is and of what he is becoming. This unveiling of his endlessly diverse personality is what the creation, especially the making of the human race is all about.

When the Bible says, *'Then God said, "Let us make man in our image, according to our likeness"',*[2] it makes this purpose clear. People are to be the revelation of God, the truth about the eternal almighty one. So the truth about humans is that we were made, men and women, to be the truth about God.

'So God created man in his own image, in the image of God he created him; male and female he created them.'[3]

49

Male and female are words describing sexual roles. It is hard for us as fallen creatures, products of the world after the great rebellion in Eden, to understand what sex must have been before the rebellion – our view of it as of all things, is horribly perverted. But we know this; sex is an expression of God's concern that man should not be alone. It is part of the total, self-sacrificing, permanent commitment known as cleaving which makes two different people *'one flesh'*.

> *'A man leaves his father and his mother and cleaves to his wife and they become one flesh. And the man and his wife were both naked, and were not ashamed.'*[4]

This is the moment when the story of humanity becomes personal – it puts on the faces of a man and woman. Whatever your opinions about evolution, special creation, modified evolutions; this is the point where the general becomes particular, we meet an individual Adam, and know that he is 'special'; and we view Eve the mother of the race and wish we could have seen her in innocence and splendour, woman before the fall.

Humans, naked and unafraid
Look at the glorious description of their relationship – 'they were both naked' and that word 'naked' is very big; there were no barriers between them. There was no fear of strength, no despising of weakness, but a mutual rejoicing in beauty, giving and receiving of honour and right worship. Different in function they were equals in status because the terrible barrier that was to come between them after the rebellion was as yet unknown. What was possible to them was a joining of body, mind and spirit that went down to the depths of their beings. And all this was untainted by guilt. *'They were not ashamed.'*

'Shame' is a terrible word. It speaks of the awful guilt that we all feel, guilt for what we have done, guilt for what we should have done, guilt for what our race has done.

Shame is what we feel when that guilt is spelt out ruthlessly, clearly, before us. But they felt none of it, they were free. When Adam first looked on Eve and rejoiced in the perfection of her breasts and the beauty of her hair he was not a voyeur. When she rejoiced in the worship of his eyes and the strength of his thighs she was not debased. Together they were beginning the revelation of the creator God that was to come through humankind.

The God revealed in the image is a composite person strangely three-cornered, for out of the cleaving was to come offspring. It may be that here is the first hint of God as Trinity.

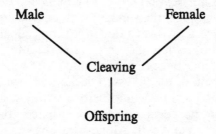

To be truly human, we must choose
But with all their beauty and perfection they were not yet what they were meant to be, not yet perfected. Something remained undetermined. They were made in the image of God and that meant free – no one ever yet bound the creator. They were free, they had to be, if they were ever to reveal the character of the living God who is becoming what he is becoming. But they could never truly reveal him unless inhabited by his life – for God is the Lord of all things. He is himself. He has no equals. But he is love, and love never forces the beloved for that would deny and destroy love itself.

Only Adam and Eve could make the choice that would join them and their heirs for ever to the living God. The tree of life stood in the centre of the garden. But there was the enemy. The Father could not deny to his children the right to hear him and choose his way if they wanted. So the tree of knowing good and evil was there with his warning. 'Do not touch it, the day you do, you will die.'

Where does Satan come from? There is no clear answer. Certainly he is one of God's high creations, fallen, twisted, perverted beyond recall. Pure spirit in rebellion, not even excused by ignorance, he can never be redeemed. He hates God, and apparently planned to use humankind as a tool in his ambition to take the throne of the universe, to turn heaven into an everlasting, cosmic torture chamber.

One thing is certain: when he offered Eve insight, knowledge and Godlike power he lied; but she was deceived by him partly because, it seems she wanted to be. Yet the situation was not beyond hope. Eve had been deceived and had disobeyed but the image was composite – it was Adam's choice that was to destroy it, or redeem it. When he looked at Eve, how did he feel? Did he feel the empty void, the distance between them, and more bitter than ever before, the pain of loneliness? Did he hope that by joining her in disobedience he would be one with her again? Taking that fruit he received the experience, the personal knowing of good and evil. Alone-ness forever.

Then the light died, the music stopped, the spirit of God was ripped away, and death came. And it is no good asking what would have been – we have no way of imagining what the world would have been if the choice had been the tree of life.

Adam's choice – Satan's reign
In that moment the godhead of this world was given to Satan – he became the object of man's worship, the tormentor of his desires the master of his reactions. The whole world was exposed to the rule of the wicked one.

God knew – how could he not know; and in the moment of darkest tragedy he made a promise, or rather a threat, because he spoke to Satan:

> *'I will put enmity between you and the woman, and between your seed and her seed; he shall bruise your head, and you shall bruise his heel.'*[5]

It was the first promise that a redeemer would come to rescue humanity from Satan's grip. But that was far in the future. The poison of estrangement entered human life and, even as God had predicted, meant the ruin of relationships – between humans and nature, person and self. But even though all seemed hopeless, the physical earth remained, in its beauty and marred harmony a testimony to the beauty of its maker.

And there was humanity made for God, hungry for something to fill that inner emptiness, sometimes fooled by Satan with false gods or phoney satisfactions. But still there were those refusing to be deceived, thirsting for the real God whom they were sure was there, beyond the boundary of the world.

All down the long years of darkness his broken heart of fatherly love followed the wanton children of men and answered those who called, while himself calling all. And the promise of the seed, the offspring, the child to come, grew stronger and clearer.

A man called Abraham and his wife Sarah became a family, a tribe, a nation, and a great people. Still the Father worked to win the **hearts** of people. Centuries passed; Covenant, Law, Judges, Kings, Prophets, Exiles, Return. Kingdom rivalled Kingdom. The empires rose and fell. Finally the iron image of Rome took centre stage. The Father was ready.

God's action, the last prophet of the old Covenant
Zechariah was tired. Old and tired. The two companion priests had left him. His solitary figure stood in the holy place. Before him was the veil that hid the Holy of Holies – the place where God's throne rested; the earthly seat of the heavenly King. The light of the seven-branched candlestick gleamed on the golden altar. Here upon live coals he spread the incense and waited till it kindled, smoke billowed, perfume ascended. He bowed and in that moment his world was upended, changed, remade.

He knew it was an angel. The wind that blew the

messenger's hair had no counterpart in the curtained stillness of the Temple and the light that shone upon him,
indeed from him, was more real, pure, radiant, more light
than any sunrise Zechariah had ever seen. But years of
disappointment had dulled the keen edge of his faith: and
even from such a messenger the news that the childless
years were over, barren Elizabeth would bear a son who
himself would be the forerunner of the Messiah, seemed
unbelievable. He said so, and paid for his folly with nine
months of silence. Deaf and dumb he waited; he was to
speak only after he had given the name of John to the child.

And what a man the child grew to be! Something wild,
glorious and free lived in him from earliest days. He was
holy, but not with the bleak icy holiness of those who
carefully calculated the merits of a tealeaf given to God.
His was the high holiness of life in love with the Lord of
hosts. 'The Baptist' they called him, because his burning
heart was never satisfied till people were dipped in the river
Jordan, as a sign of repentance and forgiveness. And
always he heralded the coming one. In the darkest hour,
before the dawn when Christ the sun of God's righteousness, rose over the scene, John the Baptist burned and
shone and thousands rejoiced in his light.

Mary's choice – God's son comes
But what of the beautiful girl who was to be the mother of
the promised seed? Six months after Zechariah had emerged from the ancient sanctity of the Temple's grandeur his
eyes filled with a vision of living holiness, she also met the
messenger; in Nazareth. There is a beauty about her, even
now, as we read her story first written nineteen hundred
years ago. That beauty is the serenity, joy and calm of a girl
who has learned to walk with her God. Not even the
appearance of Gabriel breaching the veil that hides heavenly reality from earthly shadows could make her afraid.
Only the seeming extravagance of his greeting troubled
her. As the proclamation of the great King to come from
her womb is made, she accepts his divine origin, his royal

destiny and the eternity of his reign. Only one question is asked. 'How will this happen?'

> *'The Holy Spirit will come upon you, and the power of the Most High will overshadow you; therefore the child to be born will be called holy, the Son of God.'*[6]

All the bounding, sweet, wild, holy power of God is pouring into her in those words. With quiet grace and simple calm this teenage girl ponders the will of the Father, knowing it will mean small town gossip, scandal and the life-long ruin of her reputation. The long history of the Father's loving and planning all trembled in the balance of this young girl's answer. How gentle is our God. *'I am the Lord's servant. May it happen to me as you have said.'* All of heaven must have exploded with joy at those words. The promise was fulfilled: The everliving son, the one word, the outshining of the all-creating God, became a single cell in his own creation – an ovum in the womb of a woman. God had come. The Word became flesh.

Jesus' choice – the Kingdom comes

He called himself *'son of man'* knowing that some would not clearly understand and that others understanding would be outraged. It was a title that dated from the time of Daniel – some said the son of man would be the Messiah, others that he was the ideal human, still others believed he would be the righteous redeemer. Nobody it seems thought that maybe all of them could be true. Adam's choice had been: My will, not God's. Jesus was the first human to say and totally live: *'Not my will but yours.'* Long after his resurrection Paul was to call him the second Adam, the beginner of a new race of people born to live as he lived, spiritually alive, holy and free.

The repeated theme 'good news of the kingdom of God' was constant in all his preaching. He had come to announce at last the lifting of the long satanic domination and to demonstrate it by his life. He was able to say *'the kingdom of God is among you'* because he stood among them, the incarnation of that kingdom. To the scribes and Pharisees with their incessant seeking for new minutiae of ritual law with which to bind themselves, he was a menace. It was not that he was a law breaker, it was simply that he lived so high above and beyond the law that it was irrelevant. And of course that annoyed them, particularly when it interfered with the smooth ritual of synagogue services.

Jesus' choice – release to religious captives

Eighteen years is a long time to be bent almost double with curvature of the spine. As she sat in the synagogue listening to the young rabbi on this Sabbath, her pain was worse than usual so that she could not lift her eyes to see him. Then people around her gasped. She understood when she saw feet, a man's feet in the woman's section of the synagogue. He was standing right by her and then the voice spoke again. 'Lady you are freed from your illness.' Hands touched her head with gentle authority and incredibly a demonic tension was banished, muscles regained their old strength and normal position, her spine straightened, she stood upright and began to praise and thank God. She would have understood the lines beloved by Martin Luther King: 'Free at last, free at last. Praise God almighty, I'm free at last.'

The synagogue president was furious as were his cronies: 'Disgusting. Get healed during the week, not on a sabbath.' The eyes that had warmed her with compassion now flashed with deep hidden fire. 'Actors! You would untie a donkey to water it on the sabbath. Isn't it right to untie this woman, bound by Satan for eighteen years, **on the Sabbath?**' They had no answer and slunk away in shame.

I remember hearing about a dear old man in a Brethren assembly in Devon. He was in a bit of a rut. Each week he would stand up in the Sunday morning meeting to pray and his prayer invariably started, 'Oh Lord, we've been caught in the webs of sin, its sticky lines have ensnared us...' Week after week it continued until one Sunday a forthright character decided he had had enough of the 'webs of sin'. The prayer began as usual; had reached the end of the first sentence when a stentorian voice boomed out, 'Oh Lord, **kill that spider!**'

Jesus's choice – *'Not my will'*

That's what Jesus came to do, at least to rob the spider of his power. The real battleground was his character. The proclamation and the miracles were part of the battle but the place where the victory had to be won was in his own person. As his popularity with the great mass of people began to level off, so enemies within the political and religious establishment began to push forward. The plotters surrounded Jesus with spies and *agents provocateurs*. The atmosphere in which he moved became full of suspicion and intrigue. Yet he loved them. He answered their dangerous questions with courtesy and honesty, constantly amazing them with replies that turned their tiny worlds upside down.

The cross had always stood as a dark shape on the edge of his consciousness. But now as time grew shorter and the event drew nearer the full horror of it invaded all his being. Hearing the easy triumphalism of the apostles, he trembled for them, tried to prepare them as time and time again he described what would happen to him. But they could not hear him for they would not listen or receive such thoughts. Even on the way to the Last Supper they were still arguing over the distribution of cabinet posts in Jesus' new world government.

The fact that at the Passover feast not one of them was able to humble himself to wash the feet of the others, including Jesus, was a terrifying measure of their failure to absorb even a tiny part of the vast body of teaching he had given over three years. Still more frightening to him, in his love for them, was the easy boasting confidence of their protested loyalty.

'You will betray me,' he said.

'We will never let you down, even if we should die with you.'

'These others may fall away, I never will.'

The demons must have laughed, and taunted Jesus with their jeering mockery of his manifest failure.

The last attempt to reach Judas failed as he made the fateful decision to retreat from truth. Judas went out into the night and never saw light again. All the disciples would betray, desert and deny him and Peter worst of all. The agony he felt was partly for them; he loved them still.

Jesus' choice – *'your will be done'*

He was alone, alone as no-one ever was, though not yet abandoned by the Father. As he knelt in the garden the issue was still the same. Would a man, a creature of flesh and blood like Adam, willingly stand in a wicked world and reverse Adam's choice, saying, 'God I love you for yourself and want not my will but yours?' There in Gethsemane he faced the cross, and battle was joined between good and evil.

Fiery torches in the garden, a traitor's kiss, a beating up, bloody fists, jeering laughter, gobbets of spit, hate-filled faces, cowardly judges, a cynical king and through it all he was silent. He said no word because to speak would have been to pile more guilt against them. He went on loving them.

Through the three Jewish trials, the only time he spoke was when the High Priest left his judge's seat and, beside himself with rage, shrieked into the face of Jesus, *'In the name of the living God I now put you on oath: Tell us if you are the Messiah, the son of God?'*

'I am, and you shall see the son of man sitting at the right hand of the Almighty and coming on the clouds of heaven.' He spoke calmly, levelly, unafraid.

It was what they had waited for. 'Blasphemy!' they shouted in delight. Their searing hatred had triumphed.

Pilate's choice – go with the flow

But he went on loving them. Even when handed over to Pilate he said nothing. Poor Pilate, a vain, weak bully of a man, politically inept and intellectually no match for those clever men Annas and Caiaphas, he tried hard to be a 'noble Roman'. Unfortunately he was slow-witted, shallow and heavy handed, often compensating for a lack of subtlety by unwise use of force. There is no doubt he tried to save Jesus Christ. There is no doubt he failed.

Stripped naked, stretched tight and tied to a pillar Jesus was scourged. Leather thongs bearing pieces of bone and metal flailed his back ripping off strips of skin, then flesh and muscle fibre. There was no legal limit to the number of blows. It stopped when the man with the scourge was exhausted. A King they had called him and crowned him with a crown made from a branch of thorns, thorns like great nails.

In all this, never forget the plan of the enemy. He wanted to break the living God who had emptied himself of power and been made flesh. He saw his greatest opportunity. The steady erosion of popularity, the turning back of many disciples, the hatred of the authorities and the desertion and betrayal by the apostles were all part of his assault on the psychology of the man. Then, utterly alone, Jesus had to face the physical agony and the spiritual desolation.

Nine o'clock in the morning. They nailed the right hand first, then the left. A loop of rope round the legs pulled down hard, a nail through the ankles. Then the cross lifted high was dropped into its socket in the ground.

Jesus' choice – *'Love your enemies'*
Every bone in the top of the body would snap out of joint yet ... *'Father forgive them they do not know what they are doing.'* He went on loving.

Muscles strained, ligaments tore, empty sockets grated, and still the heart pumped the life round the obscenely distended body. The cleverest twist of Satan's knife was the coming of the mother – still beautiful, serene in her trust, she was to receive today the *'sword to pierce your own heart'* promised by Simeon years ago in the Temple.

'Lady go home with John: John treat her as your mother.'

Gently, courteously, he told her, 'I am not coming home anymore.' Gently, courteously, with love he broke her heart.

Just before mid-day one of the thieves fell silent – the other continued babbling curses. Then the quiet one rebuked his companion. 'We are getting what we deserve. He has done no wrong. Jesus remember me when you come as King.' After three hours of insult that is quite a request!

'I promise you, today you will be with me in Paradise.' What a man! What a glorious man! If, in such extreme pain, he could love a man who had treated him so badly then his love was the shining radiance of God. It still is.

Jesus' choice – obey God at all costs

Twelve o'clock. Mid-day. Darkness descended; a darkness to frighten people. Maybe an eclipse and all the residue of light blotted out by rolling banks of cloud. Whatever it was, the darkness continued for three hours. In those hours the Father apparently reached backward and forward in human history to take the very essence of each one of us and place that essence in Christ. Jesus accepted us, identified with us, became one with us. In doing so he accepted our dark side, our sin. So in the darkness the Father accused the son of sin, all sin, every sin, and every consequence: Sickness, disease, famine, war, divorce, drug addiction and death. Every nasty, filthy, deceitful, greedy, lustful trick; whether hidden or open, committed in word, thought or deed, all our defilements were piled on him and he became defilement.

Now made filthy with our sin, rotten and stinking in the nostrils of a holy God, he was fitted no longer for heaven but for hell. In this awful moment the relationship between the everlasting Father and the eternal son was ripped apart; and the son fell away, down, down into the abyss. Grinning shallowness, cruel idiocy, rapacious nothingness closed around him. The King of heaven languished a captive in hell.

'My God, my God, why have you abandoned me?' The

cry of desolation echoed round the hills, no answer came, none was possible. It was the loneliest moment ever. It was for you and me. The ransom was paid. He had paid the price of our release from Satan's clutches.

Jesus' obedience – God's victory

Satan had failed! In the moment of seeming victory he had lost: The grinding pressure he had applied to the son of man had provoked no sin nor selfishness, exposed no pride, only love. Satan, whose only right was to hold the guilty, the sinner in his kingdom, had slain the innocent.

'*I thirst,*' he said but wanted nothing they could give him. Thirst is the perpetual state of hell. He had plumbed its bottomless deep, but there was nothing in him to hold him there. The account was fully paid. And so we hear still echoing down the centuries the great cry, '*It is accomplished.*'

The innocent Maker had died for his guilty creations and henceforth any of them could claim his sacrifice for their release. From that moment in our space and time, I was forgiven and so were you. We need only receive him. Life for life, loyalty for loyalty: Accept him and we change sides in life's great war.

God's victory – humans remade

Breathing '*Father, into your hands I commit my Spirit,*' he surrendered the life he had put on in the womb. Because he did, we can find new life. Born again, we step into his kingdom. The kingdom of God's dear son. We live in this world as he did, in the plan of the Father, in the will of the King. So, as the plan unfolds we find the truth of what Jesus said: '*I said, you are gods ... to whom the word of God came.*'[7] Humans like gods – at last! When they saw he was dead, they decided to check. So, just to make sure, they pierced his side with a spear. The blood and water that came out not only proved his death, it makes it almost certain he had died of a ruptured heart. What a picture God gives us of himself, nail-pierced, thorn-crowned, heart-broken; God really is **love**.

By the sacrifice of Jesus we can be loosed from the chains of guilt and set free to live, by love, the life which God planned for us from eternity. That purpose has never changed. Still God loves you and wants you to live for him in a way that no one else ever could. The cross of Calvary has made it possible for you to enter your destiny and really live.

Our choice – to be made new
Will you take some time to reflect on the foulness of sin, God's holiness and therefore the deep love that took Jesus Christ from the heights of heaven to the depths of hell; all because he was determined you should accomplish your purpose? It might be appropriate to be very glad about it! Give him thanks. The following prayer may help:

> 'Lord Jesus Christ as I look at your cross
> I am amazed at your love. You did not have to do it.
> But you died for me, for all of us.
> I worship you as perfect man and loving God
> Thank you for taking my faults into your body on the
>   cross.
> I give you every sin, guilt and failure.
> Thank you for forgiving me, for making me clean.
> Thank you. Thank you.
> Help me to walk always in the cleansing light of your
>   sacrifice.
> Amen.'

For many people the story of Calvary is the whole gospel; but it is not – it is the doorway to the real thing. The Lord has opened the door so let us go right on in . . .

Chapter 5

Discipleship – Anything Can Happen

Serving the living Lord – in the power of the Spirit
As we watched, jets streaked over the target area, security buildings sank into predetermined places in bomb-proof bunkers, a missile flashed to its target, a giant oil drilling platform toppled slowly into the waiting sea. Suddenly a Hollywood epic voice snarled, 'Anything can happen in the next half-hour!'

The next episode of *Stingray* was under way. 'Anything can happen...' It was rarely true, of course. Usually the adventures of the life-like puppets were comfortably predictable; like church? At least, that is the way we seem to want it to be!

'What happened at church this morning?'

'Oh. Nothing much. Same as usual.'

That conversation should be impossible. For with God **nothing** is impossible. Something must happen and almost anything can. 'All things are possible.' As C.S. Lewis put it in the Narnia books, 'Aslan is not a tame lion.' We deal with a **living** God. And because he lives, we should live also. But so often we allow circumstances around us, our own digestions or satanic pressure to rob us of his presence. Like the two on the road to Emmaus, we walk with heads bowed, voices low and faces downcast. Our feet drag, misery trails behind us. What a state – we almost deserve to be called *'of all men most miserable'*. Jesus still asks as he did then, *'What are you talking about, as you walk along?'*

The sadness showed as they looked at him! 'You must be the only man in Jerusalem who doesn't know the things that have been happening.'

'What things?' he asked.

Pain hung in the air as they talked about the innocent one, condemned and cruelly slaughtered by a cynical alliance between Jewish religion and Roman power. Confusion also as they told him of the dead man not allowed to rest decently in his tomb; the grave opened, strange messengers and hysterical women. They told of men sent to investigate but *'him they did not see'*. They were talking about the right things, the things of God, but with the wrong attitude.

'Brainless and slow-hearted. Don't you see? It was **necessary** for the Christ to suffer that way and enter into his splendour.' Then he started; taking them back to the beginning, to Adam and then on a lightning tour through the Old Testament. Overturning all their previous thinking which was petty, parochial, earthbound, he showed them the mighty plan of God and 'Christ the Tiger' in the centre of it. He stretched their Jewish frame and set them in a cosmic context.

How long did it take to walk those seven miles: Three, maybe four hours. Their eyes were opened and excitement gripped them. Yet not till he broke the bread in the house did they recognise him. Then he was gone.

We walk in the power of the Holy Spirit
Now watch them – they dash back to Jerusalem, run up the steps, burst into the upper room, start to say, 'We have seen him! Jesus is alive,' only to be met by, 'We know! Peter has seen him.' Glorious anti-climax! They were transformed because they met the resurrection Christ. But by his direct command they were prevented from going out to spread the good news. For he planned a gospel bigger than just **talking** about his own resurrection. The gospel they were to proclaim was the sharing of his resurrection, and they could not do this until they had the reality in their

experience. 'Wait' he said, 'until the power from above comes down upon you ... In a few days you will be baptised in the Holy Spirit.'

Quick! Form ranks in party lines! Back to the trenches! Theological grenades at the ready: Fire!

Pentecostal!
Liberal!
Experientialist!
Doctrinalist!
Modernist!
Traditionalist!
Charismatic!
Non-Charismatic!
Instamatic!
Automatic!
Rheumatic!
Aromatic!

Well, now we have dispersed with the formalities per-haps we can think about the phrase. After all, something, which the Bible reports as being said by John the Baptist four times,[1] the apostle Peter,[2] the apostle Paul[3] and Jesus himself[4] cannot be all bad!

Baptism: To the Greeks the simple act of dipping any-thing in water or other liquid so that it is completely washed, and thoroughly saturated – sometimes a shirt in a bowl of dye. Used by the Jews to describe the act of repentance when a man was dipped in a river or lake to publicly admit his sin and need of washing by God. Christ-ians took it over and filled it with more meaning. Desire for cleansing moved repentance and faith that committed them to Jesus Christ as Saviour and Lord, then later, to the trinity God.

We live in the fullness of the Holy Spirit
So it was the moment of change; the point in life where a man was buried with Christ and raised in the power of his resurrection. It was the moment when the old principle of

independent action was laid in the grave and the new principle of obedience to the Holy Spirit was established. Death to the old man, life from Jesus Christ.

Out of Eden flowed four rivers, their names – Freely flowing, Stream, Arrow-swift, Bursting with sweetness – form a beautiful picture of a river of life. Ezekiel saw a river flowing from the Temple. Wherever it went new life came. First it was ankle deep, then knee deep, thigh deep and finally *'deep enough to swim in'*. Jesus promised we should have *'rivers of living water'* which John said was a promise about the gift of the Holy Spirit.

Do you see the picture? The Holy Spirit of God is the outpoured torrent of the life of God – bubbling, effervescing, it fountains out of him then streams away from him. And this wild, sweet, holy river is a person of beauty, splendour and divine authority. He is glorious to know and given to us. He is the guarantee of the resurrection. We give Christmas presents but Jesus gave us the resurrection/ascension present of his spirit as our share in his triumph.[5]

If you are in Christ, the Spirit of God is yours! But the reality of the gift may be held from your experience; first because you have not understood that he is given as a gift, freely.

> *'How much more will the heavenly Father give the Holy Spirit to those who ask him!'*[6]

It may be that you have never reached out and **received** by faith what God has already given. God wants to make real in your experience the blessings which are given to you by his promise. Secondly, because the Holy Spirit is the Lord, you will fail to know his fullness if you do not live in continuing obedience to him. This is an essential key to being filled with the Holy Spirit. But since no one is perfect yet, we all falter in our obedience; we need the grace of repentance. This is the other key to fullness.

We live in obedience to the Holy Spirit
So, returning to the phrase, 'Baptism in the Spirit', must at least mean being buried and raised again in the Spirit. Its

reality will not come until in a true meeting with the divine authority of the Holy Spirit of God, each of us surrenders the central citadel of our will.

Such a moment may or may not be a great crisis. It may or may not be attended by great emotional explosions. But it will be a moment when the sovereignty of God enters and takes over from the sovereignty of self. At last the river of God's life begins to flow into, through and out of a human being and we are back to the original principle of Eden. Though fallen creatures in a fallen world we have begun to live by eating from the tree of life.

As we move in obedience to the prompting of the Holy Spirit, the Father is able to start unfolding the pattern of his destiny for us. Living under his Lordship we are free! Just like a bird in the air, a fish in water or a horse on the open downs we are free because a man or a woman living in the Spirit, is living in his or her natural element.

> *'Now the Lord is the Spirit and where the Spirit of the Lord is, there is freedom.'*[7]

This is not freedom to sin but freedom to do the will of God – to find his plan and live it out. It means freedom to live a life that is pure, holy and disciplined, not because somebody passed a law that says I ought to be those things, but because I know my destiny is to be like Christ and the person of the Holy Spirit within me draws me on to the will of God and gives me power to do it.

The alternative – to live in bondage
Those who will not live by this principle are doomed to live under life-denying laws: rules and regulations constantly proliferating as people seek to explain them more fully. Bound up, tensed up, miserable people are the result, a barren, powerless, stereotyped existence. Or, of course, one can decide that the keeping of so many rules is imposs-ible and start to live in a spurious freedom. Spurious because anything that gives me the right to sin actually

brings me into terrible bondage. Loose, feckless and spiritually dull I become a walking advertisement for Christian boredom.

I was meant for better things. For a start I am a child of God, not a robot. A robot functions automatically according to a set of predetermined instructions, but a child of a loving Father is free, free to laugh, to cry, free to feel joy and anger within the Father's arms. The emotions are unbound, because in the trusting relationship with the Father the child can expose all the pains, hurts, joys, bitterness, excitements and agonies of his or her heart. Happy man – or woman – who lives like this. There is a deep, secure happiness that comes from knowing we have shown the deepest hurts and the very worst in us to God and still he loves us. But because this is true freedom it is dangerous. We have the right to participate in God's purpose for us. However, in addition we have the right to disobey, to get out of God's scheme. We may thus become part of the many who stagnate and die respectably. As an American clergyman said at a funeral: 'Brothers and sisters, this corpse has been a member of this church for forty years!'

If you are one of those who are asleep in Christ, then 'Wake up. Wake up sleeper. Rise from the dead. Christ waits to bless you with Light.'

Alternatively, we may backslide into spectacular disobedience and force God to let us learn the truth of the phrase 'miserable as sin'.

The road home – repentance

Maybe you have done that already and are reading this in a 'far-off country'. Listen to God's voice. His plan for you is not static and immovable. It is dynamic, organic; steadily unfolding in a way that is flexible. Make a mistake and the Father will incorporate it in the plan, provided you commit the mistake, the sin to him. The only voice that tells you, 'It's all over. You've really blown it. You'll never be any good as a Christian now,' is a satanic one. The Father sees you even when you are a long way away, and if you start to come home, he runs to meet you, flings his arms around you and holds you. You may have made some wrong choices – give them to him. Surrender 'second best' in repentance to him and he will work on it. He will forge it into 'best' in the white heat of his holiness.

As a child of God called to a destiny that is yours alone, you have to beware of Satan's power to use 'the enemy within'. You **cannot** be defeated by any other power that comes against you from outside. But when an impregnable fortress is fast locked against an enemy, the clever attacker gets a traitor inside the castle to open the doors. And Satan is clever.

A young trainee minister was preaching a sermon before the Principal of his college, C.H. Spurgeon. Firmly he expounded Ephesians 6, putting on the armour of God. Helmet of salvation, breastplate of righteousness, shield of faith and all the other equipment was enthusiastically donned. Then he asked with ringing rhetoric:

'And now where are you, Satan?'

Spurgeon leaned forward over the balcony and shouted, 'Inside the armour.'

The unholy trinity

Satan has three special areas of temptation in us, an unholy trinity of weakness where too often he receives ready welcome: Misuse of sex (lust), love of things/money (materialism), and self-centredness (pride). If he is not going to rob you of the crown that Jesus wants to give you, you must go to war against his control in these areas of your life.

The Holy Spirit – the power of Jesus' resurrection – is given to you to make you holy, a true disciple. Holiness and discipline begin with understanding that God has a special purpose for you, a purpose that will never be fulfilled if not by you.

(i) **Lust:** If God has planned for you to meet and marry a certain person, you do not have the right to deprive that person of the blessing of your love (doubtful blessing though you may feel it to be). You are made for someone special so do not give yourself to someone else. Remember too, sex is made to happen inside marriage. Marriage is a commitment made by God to protect sex, because he wants us to enjoy our sexuality. Sex used simply as passing entertainment turns sour and destroys the real humanity of people who use it. Sex outside of marriage between people who love each other and intend to marry, is destructive of their present relationship and future stability. Research into divorce statistics bears this out. If the woman/man you love is the one intended for you from eternity then be prepared to demonstrate your love for them by enduring the pain of waiting – **that** will prove that you love them! For pain is the measure of love. If he or she is not the one meant for you, then don't play games – people who play games with sex find themselves scarred by its corrosive power. Like a powerful chemical, sex needs a strong purpose-built container – marriage. Get it in that container used by the people for whom it is intended and the explosions of ecstasy may be heard all over creation!

'How do I know who is right for me?' people ask. Answer: we can marry any one we like provided they are single, in Christ and of the opposite sex. We should look for someone who is seeking God's kingdom and wanting the continuing fullness of his Spirit. Then for a coinciding of interests, growing friendship and a meeting of minds and spirits. If those things are there the next will be right, if we seek God and his kingdom. He will guide us by his Holy Spirit poured into us. He wants us to be happy. That is why he calls us to sexual purity. There is a joy in chastity that we will not know if we are not chaste. We can never know the high holy joy of only ever having one sexual partner and that one within marriage if we throw away our purity in a series of stupid sexual adventures. Your virginity is a marvellous gift from God, don't let anyone take it from you. Marriage is the holy place where you yield that gift to the one for whom it is intended.

True love waits

Yes, of course, I know that this is a high standard and almost impossible. We will never begin to master this area unless we clearly understand the nature of personal destiny. You see, if God has plans for you and me, then we matter too much to throw it all away. 'We love each other too much to wait,' we say, reluctant to recognise one of the mind's most appealing con-tricks. It is not 'loving too much' but 'not loving enough'. Real love would say 'I will never ask the beloved to do what is wrong. No matter what pain I feel. I will endure it with joy because of the love I feel for them.' Real love would only ask the loved one to do what is right. Could anyone ask someone else for whom God has a special individual destiny and meaning to obscure and defile that purpose, and say 'I acted in love'? No way. But we do. And whether Christian or agnostic, in reflective moments we are able to recognise that often the longing for gratification 'now' has overwhelmed our knowledge of what is best for the relationship. We have lost sight of the individual; the person before us has become a commodity, sometimes regarded as little more than a recreational facility. Purity in sexual relations turns on the recognition of the important nature of each individual made in God's image for his purpose. The way forward is to ask God for **real** love: The kind of love that loves the other person too much to do what is wrong.

We do live in a sex-orientated culture and this generation is specially pressurised. But Jesus has encouragement for us – he knows how difficult it is to stand up for him, his standards and his words, in a sexually loose generation. So he makes it clear there are special blessings for those who do it. He will give a special sense of identity, purpose and spiritual authority.

Probably more of us are conscious of failure in this area than any other. I know what it is to try again and again, and to fail. There is only one answer – confess your sin, receive forgiveness and go on. I want to encourage you because I have experienced the power of Christ's resurrection in this.

I was once an adulterer – Christ has purified me. I know his Holy Spirit can make a dirty man clean, he has done it for me. I was bound, helpless before my lust. Through years of struggle he sustained me, then set me free. To which I can only add, 'Thank God.' No matter how often we fall, we are still called to purity. So let us obey the King. We can live in freedom.

(ii) Materialism: Just as sexual sin is a natural outworking of materialism so also is the love of things and money. Love of things creeps upon us so quietly and gradually. It is a good respectable sin fitting itself uniquely to working class culture, middle class preferences and upper crust indulgence. At its most noble this sin surfaces in the love of nature, especially in artistic and romantic people. They can so easily find themselves swept along by the love of mountains and valleys, rivers and lakes, that beautiful views will move them to make a god of nature.

The pronouncements of some environmentalists come close to this sort of idolatry. In fact some parts of the 'Green' faction make it clear that for them Mother Earth is the only deity worth bothering with. They are mistaken. The earth and sky with all their wonders are meant to lead us in worship to the unseen God who is author of them. There is also the danger that someone who enjoys physical activity such as climbing or fell-walking may be led by their love of the hills into a false dichotomy: 'I feel I can know God better out in the hills than sitting in a stuffy old church.' True and untrue. It will be true of certain specific occasions but as a general principle it is simply a deception.

The earth was given to the human race in the beginning. It was given to be our possession, a possession held in trust. Adam was made steward of the earth and told to have dominion over it – he was commanded to have a working relationship with it. He was not to worship it, he was to reign over it as God's ambassador. We were not made for the earth, the earth was made for us. We are to take care of it precisely because it was made for us, as our home. So we should never worship anything made from the earth nor bow down to it. That is a blasphemy. Our consumer society is a blasphemous society precisely because it is **thing**-centrèd.

Increasing numbers of people go to work, not to provide for families but to buy more things. Jesus called it *'serving mammon'*. We hear increasing numbers of couples agreeing to have no children because they do not want 'messy kids' spoiling their beautiful homes and possessions. Serving mammon. And we Christians are so easily swept along with the rest of our blasphemous society in an unspoken worship of the products of the transistor and the silicon chip. Powerful cars smoothly accelerating away from the opposition; television sets so big and vivid that they are more real than real-life; ovens that think for you, washing machines that do everything except play 'Blue Danube'; hi-fi equipment that is 'better than being there'; and gadgets galore; pay your money, bow down and worship; if you want to die inside. For with all their glitter things bring sadness as they decay, bondage when they are threatened and death when we are tied to them.

God's gift, our pleasure

Now all the things we can make from the earth are for us to enjoy. Nothing is bad in itself, and God gives us richly all things to enjoy. And we will enjoy them provided we do not regard any possessions as ours in any real sense. We need to step back from our possessions and realise they are gifts, gifts from God. Then we will be free from them and truly able to enjoy them. That is our destiny, to be free from the love of things and so, able to accept it cheerfully when they get spoilt, broken or destroyed. Ultimately things do not matter. We should enjoy what God gives as an expression of his goodness. But let us hold our possessions loosely so that when they are gone our hearts do not chase after them, but stay at home in God.

Our society is very covetous and, therefore, generosity is not something that comes easily to us. In recent years the

73

sense of being in decline has made us meaner than we have ever been in our history, which has affected the Church. The British church in the last few years has an appalling record in the area of giving. So let us learn generosity: By giving money away until it hurts. Next time you are faced with a request for funds in the kingdom of God, dare to ask God what you should give. Assess each situation. Listen to his voice and then give what he says even if it seems too much! You see, nobody else can give your money away – that is your destiny and privilege. Dare to give away more than ever before. There are few things so exciting or liberating as giving money away. It is a delightfully anarchistic thing to do in our greedy society!

In addition to such private action we need to help those who take collective action to challenge the selfish assumptions of our society. The steady demolition by the Government of our welfare system may make fiscal sense but only in the short term. When the structures erected to care for the poor, weak, and sick are destroyed to save money for the prosperous; the message is clear: Such people are disposable. No wonder the apprentice thugs on our streets feel the old and sick are fair game.

(iii) Pride: What do we do about it? Sometimes it is obvious, more often it is subtle and all the more dangerous. The fact is 'I' like reigning over 'my' life. Even when I know that it is making me miserable I hang on, desperately trying to maintain my hold on the controls. But it is not what I am called to. And here the principle of individual destiny cuts right across my rebellion, and yours.

Without a clear sense of God's purpose for you there is a grave danger that you will determine the way ahead on your own. You may feel that is all right, even for a Christian. But if you accept that God has a plan for each individual the priority becomes the discovery of his will, not yours. God's will then confronts your will and you have a fight on your hands. The Spirit of God wrestles with your spirit to bring it into obedience to Christ because the King of kings wants you to reign in life. But you can only do that when he reigns in you. He has to be your King before you can have his kingly authority. He confronts the rebellious heart and demands obedience.

Humility

Humility is a rare but beautiful thing. It is the fruit of dependence and obedience. The only way to be truly humble is to surrender freely to the Lord and obey Him. If you are ever to be really happy you must surrender to his destiny for you. You were not made to run your own life without his authority as the King – for without his authority over you there is no authority in you. He is the most splendid conqueror the world has ever known, for he wins by loving. Nobody but he has earned the right to reign over you. The scars in his hands and feet and side are his pledge to you of love that goes to hell and back. The wounded God who died of a broken heart because of his love for you only has one desire: that you should be what you are meant to be – free.

We live in the freedom of the Spirit

As his Holy Spirit pours through these areas of life cleansing and conforming them to his pattern, freedom will increasingly be ours. Freedom not to sin. Freedom to do what is right and so freedom to really live in life, and for Life himself to live in us.

That means we will enter that priceless treasure and privilege, our true selves. The individual adventure of God's own life will go out into the earth to reveal itself in our flesh and blood. For in all these things we will know God differently from anyone else, and the revelation we receive will be seen by others. Your life is an unrepeatable opportunity. It is a work of art that will be created once only. You are not a photographic reproduction, but an artist's original. Therefore, you must live what, where and when no one ever lived before. Do not let fear hold you back. The Lord is with you.

'Lord God, thank you for the privilege of being me.
Give me the guts to take hold of your grace.
Give me the courage to enter your holiness.
Make me the person you want me to be. Amen.'

Remember those words from *Star Trek*: 'To boldly go where no one has gone before'? That is your calling and you have something far better than the Starship 'Enterprise' – you have the Lord of life, the Holy Spirit, in you. The power that raised Jesus from the dead in the dimension of space and time and seated him on the throne of power in the eternal dimension of the heavens can certainly carry you 'where no one has gone before'. So boldly go...

... into the next chapter? There, gutsy guys and C.T. Studd await us.

Chapter 6

Godliness with Guts

The challenge of discipleship – for men

'The men in the church are so wet! Where are the real men?'

What would you have said? 'Outside the church'; 'On the sports field', or 'down the pub'? I tried to find an adequate answer but the question continued to haunt me. In fact, it was asked by other people in different forms – and still I could find no answer. Gutlessness was the indictment: an angry Christian girl charged the men of the western church with being effete, self-indulgent, soft-living, comfort-loving, unable to endure hardness. And because of this they were also described as being incapable of commanding respect, even from their own wives and families.

What makes a 'real man'? Is it bulging biceps, a chiselled chin and the throaty roar of a sports car? Do we write off every skinny weak-chinned cyclist as a hopeless non-runner in the manhood stakes?

The answer to those questions is so obviously 'no'. The evidence of history and our own knowledge of people is that all too often big muscular physical types can be soft and self-indulgent. Samson is a superb example of a man who was 'all man' yet not a real man, for his indiscipline prevented him from ever saying 'no' to his own desires and feelings. He was crippled by his refusal to face the implications of his own destiny: called to be God's servant, a warrior of heaven, he would not allow his life to be governed by heavenly principles. He really thought he could be soft on himself, and he paid a dreadful price.

The call to discipline

It seems clear that the quality that marks out a real man is the ability to be hard on himself, to deny himself. This quality becomes more obvious when the hardness is for the sake of a purpose outside himself, particularly if it is clear that the purpose is bigger than he is. No longer bound by the considerations of his own comfort he is a man living for a cause; and the better the cause the better the man will become because we tend to take on the character of what we serve.

Serving Christ we have the exhilarating experience of a cause that is of ultimate importance; everything we do has significance for eternity. All of life matters. Only give a man that cause to live and work for. Assure him of his destined place in the outworking of the everlasting purpose of God, and even the most spineless of 'eight stone weaklings' becomes a courageous, determined 'man of destiny'! He is undefeatable and indefatigable. The gifts of identity and purpose, fit him to be what he is meant to be, God's gift to the Church and the world. He has become a 'real man' for he is a man with a cause. The men of the early Church were men with a cause.

The call to courage

The cripple was healed, not much doubt about it. He had danced and jumped his way up the steps and into the Temple, his shouts of happiness attracting a huge crowd. Then Peter had immediately taken advantage of the scene by proclaiming the authority of Jesus the Christ once crucified, now risen from the dead. Of course, the priests were outraged: Peter and John were soon arrested. After a night in the cells to cool their ardour they were arraigned for trial before the whole Jewish establishment. Completely unabashed, Peter the fisherman from Galilee set about putting them on trial instead: *'Jesus Christ of Nazareth whom you crucified has healed the man you now see before you.'* Astonished at such outspokenness, the priests thought there was only one explanation for the boldness displayed by Peter and John – uneducated common men (literally ungrammatical idiots!) – they had been with Jesus.

These men were gutsy, gritty characters whose courage in living had so obviously come from an encounter with the man Jesus. He had proved impossible to deal with and now it seemed that his followers would be like him! For they had come away from the encounter with not only a sense of the importance of the message, but also with a certainty of their own part in its proclamation. Remember that moment by Galilee when Peter knelt amongst an unbelievably large catch of fish and said, *'Go away from me, Lord, I am too sinful'*? Jesus did not deny the fact of Peter's sin, only the conclusion he reached. 'Don't be afraid,' he said. It may seem that a sinful man dares too much when he enters the service of God – it is worse for him to allow fear to stop him. Do not dare not to dare.

So many western Christians, men and women, have forgotten that each of us has been commissioned by the risen Christ to bear his message out into the world. We do not have to apologise for our presence, or our message, only for our ineffectiveness in communicating it. We should always tackle life and witness with confidence, and sometimes with aggression, never timidity. There is a place for the fighting spirit. Unfortunately, few of our warriors are using the fighting spirit in the right direction. Too often we are fighting each other while the battle for the proclamation of the gospel and the relief of suffering goes by default. Much of our preaching would also be improved by an injection of aggression. Too rarely we hear preaching that is designed to send troops out into the war against selfishness, injustice and demonic evil, with the idea that we are actually on the winning side and our contribution in the war is vital to victory. God give us preachers who make Jesus real – he is the source of Christian courage.

Jesus, the human face of God
Earlier we looked at Jesus as a sort of spiritual version of
the Milky Bar Kid, a rather weak, ineffective, even effeminate 'nice' man; an idea that is responsible, more than
anything else, for the desperately low level of attainment
amongst Christian manhood. We must, therefore, be sure
that in knowing Jesus we are knowing the real Jesus – the
authentic New Testament Christ – to whom the **common**
people listened with delight: The Jesus who made people
laugh with suggestions that they feed sons on a lump of
rock, or with a snake instead of a fish; who could parody
the pompous, self-congratulations of a Pharisee at prayer,
who could raise the dead and then arrange for the one
raised to have something to eat; who on an urgent journey
could stop to ask a smelly old lady to talk about her life
story, including twelve years of illness, and then listen to
her tale of woe. His compassion made it impossible for him
to be unfaithful to himself by pleasing a bunch of self-
righteous, censorious, religious hypocrites in the house of
Simon the leper. Instead, he accepted the clumsy, tearful,
embarrassing repentance of a known prostitute, making
enemies for life of those powerful men.

We must return to the Jesus of the New Testament, the
real man, the flesh and blood human being who was the
only real human being who ever lived. In other words, we
must grasp again the blood and guts reality of the incarnation. In so many churches there seems to be an unspoken
understanding that the Gospels are a source of pretty stories suitable for little children and women! Such an attitude
not only devalues women and children, it robs men of the
chance to explore the mystery of manhood. Too often
ministers are tempted to pursue abstruse lines of doctrine
from the prophets to the epistles.

Manly – not macho
The Gospels must once more become the study of Christian
men who desire to know how to become that rare commodity, **manly** Christians. By the same study the women of

the church can be liberated to be womanly warriors of Christ the perfect human.

He must be our study because he was a man of courage and endurance beyond our normal notions of such things; a man who having had his back reduced to living pain-wracked mincemeat, could still carry a heavy wooden cross halfway up a hill before finally collapsing. While enduring this he carried on being what he was – he was not changed in essence by the torture. He was refined by it. His reactions were the reactions of love. This was the integrity of true manhood. Knowing he was to die a hideous death, knowing he was already maimed and reduced to something that no longer looked human, he could still turn to the women weeping with sympathy, to say, 'Don't weep for me. Weep for yourselves.' He knew the pain that was coming on them in the future and felt it more than his own present pain. That is what it really means to be a **man**. To endure all things and then to endure more, to go on and on into the darkness of death; through it, out into resurrection. And this is real holiness – the boldness of a man set apart for God's purpose and living it out. We won't learn it from anyone else but Jesus. He wants to teach us.

Happy and holy
So, there is an area of life that can be touched by the power of God only through you as **you** are. You do not know what you can do; the greatness of his power in you is immeasurable and its effectiveness is limited only by your availability. He has given you power, power beyond understanding, power for living, power to enable you to live a holy life. His eternal purpose for you is that you should be *'holy and without fault before him.'*[1] That is your destiny and he has chosen it for you because he wants you to be happy. Satan has twisted our ideas, we have confused holiness with self-righteousness. We have believed the lie that a holy man is necessarily someone who is a miserable person, an austere ascetic, a mystical other-worldly presence who with a severe smile full of lofty blessing and a

81

slight frown of disapproval, contrives to make everyone else feel guilty. There is only one answer to that picture: The name 'Jesus'. In him holiness and happiness were completely entwined: He makes it impossible to be holy without being supremely happy. For holiness is the state in which a man or woman has understood and begun to live out the plan of the Father for them – to be holy is to be set apart for God's special use – so it is the on-going state of supreme happiness. We are set apart to tell out,

> 'You are the chosen race, the King's priests, the holy nation, God's own people, chosen to proclaim the wonderful acts of God, who called you out of darkness into his own marvellous light.'[2]

Precisely! We are to tell the wonder of him, the one who called us out of darkness into his light. Not to witness to church membership, nor to correct doctrine, nor even to what he has done in general terms; we are called to witness to Jesus and what he has done for **us**. For he has snapped the chains, tearing apart the ropes that tied us in the prison of our own selfishness. He has freed us from the bondage of trying to get anywhere by keeping rules which could only condemn us. All this he has done by giving us his own life so that we become heirs of God, equipped with the power to live out our individual destiny as he lived his own unique life.

Every moment counts

So use all your time. If your life is a once-only opportunity for God to say something original then you dare not waste it. Since every second is a creative moment breathed out by God himself, then we should be disciplined and ordered in using it. But this must not be allowed to turn each moment into a torment. We are not meant to get strung-up but released into the freedom of knowing that since every min-ute matters, **everything** I do is of account to him and can be used by him if surrendered to him. The first realisation of this can be a wild heady experience of undreamt freedom. It is the way Jesus lived.

Jesus was the embodiment of the law, and its total fulfilment, but he was never **under** it. He kept it not as an unwilling slave whipped by its strictures, but as a free man living day by day in his own choices. Because he was consciously the second Adam, the son of God uniquely formed by the spirit's activity in the womb of Mary, these choices always reflected God's choices. He did what he wanted and always what he wanted was what God wanted. And this life of freedom is intended for us because we 'share the same origin'. We are born of the seed of God as he was and so nothing that was possible to Jesus is impossible to us. In theory! In practice his consistency eludes us.

Sinless perfection? No, of course not, but perfection remains the aim. *'Be ye perfect as your Father in heaven is perfect,'* is a direct command with implied promise. This faith of ours is God's own strategy for transforming ordinary fallen men and women into the likeness of Christ, and it should work. It does. By love.[3]

Love is the key
When motivated by and expressed in active passionate love, it **works**. Love is the route of God's power to us and also the result of his work in us. And since it is the heart of our relationship with him, it is the end of the law, the fulfilling of it. Asked to choose the most important text in all his Jewish Bible, Jesus picked out, *'You shall love the Lord your God with all your heart and with all your soul and with all your mind and with all your strength,'* because he said that on it and its companion, *'You shall love your neighbour as yourself ... depend all the law and the prophets'.*

Will you commit yourself to such a love? A life in love with God is exciting to live and to see. Such a life is a delight to God and a dread to Satan. The world needs more of this sort of Christianity instead of the pallid imitation produced by merely believing the right things, behaving

properly, thinking correctly and having good aims. Important though right doctrine, ethics, philosophy and ideals are,
they can only produce a colourless, characterless copy of
Christianity. Pale and ghostly, it looks enough like the real
thing to fool the world and the church, but never God. For
life to be sustained there must be a living beating heart of
love. The love God has for you can never be experienced
by anybody else, the love you give him can never come
from anybody else.

This is the meaning and purpose of all life and death. We
must sometime come to the ultimate human destination –
the cross and resurrection of Jesus; to be set free from the
bondage of sin – selfishness, egotism, lustfulness, greed etc.
– and released into loving the eternal God.

Then, comes the command *'You shall love the Lord Your
God'*, but no longer as an instrument of dread exposing our
inadequacies. Instead it releases us by the power of promise
– 'You shall'. We hear the unalterable purpose of God: this
is what we were made for, this is what we were meant to be.
The command/promise tells us how it will happen. It
exposes to us God's pattern for a lifelong process of transformation.

First, he releases us into loving him with all the **heart**,
pouring out on him the full treasure of our emotional being,
so that all other relationships naturally take a lower place.
There is a fierce burning passion for God that reduces all
idols, however dear, to ashes in its flame. Such a love has to
be expressed. When was the last time you said, 'Oh, God I
do love you'?

Then we love with all the **soul**; all that eternal, individual, spiritual essence that makes 'you' who 'you' are. By
settled determination and a voluntary act of the will consistently applied, we totally commit to him all that we are,
giving ourselves to him so completely that we no longer
belong to ourselves. Thus we find the ultimate meaning of
what we are. We become more truly ourselves and our own
than we ever were. Our identity is linked unalterably with
our relationship with God. As the relationship grows so
does our identity.

When God requires love with all the **mind**, he immediately removes Christianity far from the realm of the mystery cults so dear to many in our society today. There are
good reasons for loving him, and he expects us to think
through these just as he expects us to use our minds in
order to see him at work and understand his ways in all
things. We are not called to a mindless emotionalism, drift-
ing into sentimentality, but to be transformed in daily loving by the God-centred renewing of our minds.

Loving with all the **strength** may seem simple and
obvious and perhaps for that reason is not most obvious in
our British churches. It calls for us to apply all our physical
and mental vigour in worship — the word 'worship' meaning, giving God what he is worth.

> *'I appeal to you, therefore, brethren ... to present your
> bodies as a living—sacrifice, which is your spiritual
> (reasonable) worship.'*

Now, of course, this means in all of life, but many of us
need to learn to accept that our bodies do have a function in
worship. I am personally not one for leaping about too
much, but I long to see more vigour in our worship. I enjoy
seeing others free to express love for God with all their
strength. A preacher from this country visited a synagogue
while in New York and was present when all the men
participated in a stately circular dance. He was overwhelmed by the reality of their worship and later com-
mented, 'I was saddened as I thought of my church at home
– there was more glory under the old covenant than under
the new.'

Freedom of the King's children

Perhaps we need to learn again the lesson of sonship. I
never forget the story of Billy Bray the old Methodist
preacher who used to dance on his own in the lanes of
Cornwall, for sheer joy and constant amazement that he
was 'the King's son'.[4] The Lord came to start a new holy

nation of free people, laughing for joy, radiant in faith, secure in purpose. Living with him, constantly in the present moment, we really would be free, laughing people. God grant us to become those who live in the now with the living God who has made us his sons and daughters.

Such a vision is absolutely vital if the radical transformation needed by our churches is to ever happen. Without a clear sight of Jesus we will never have the necessary courage to change things. And without change, many churches run the risk of simply being by-passed by the moving Spirit of God. Much church life seems to be dominated largely by fear of change. It seems that the instructions of 1 Corinthians 12–14 are totally ignored in the worshipping life of so many congregations, where no opportunity is given for 'each one' to bring *'a hymn, a lesson, a revelation, a tongue or an interpretation'*[5]

Strange that those who maintain such services often quote, *'All things should be done decently and in order.'*[6] Yet there is no need for such sharing to be disorderly. And it would add a new human dimension.

Now I am not launching an attack on mainline denominational church life; I am a minister of a mainline denomination, and in my local church we are trying to work out a right place for such sharing in the formal worship. I am pleading for the courage of the Spirit of God in church life. And by doing so I am questioning all those things done simply because 'we have always done it that way'. You see, I really believe that every individual is called to know his God in a way that I never can; so every member of Christ can show me something beautiful of him. And I want to see it as only he can show it.

It is strange that among our traditional groupings 'free' churches are often more rigid in pattern than the established churches. Sometimes an unwritten liturgy is harder to change than a written one. We must have the boldness of the Lord Jesus himself if we are to change things which by familiarity and age have attained a false sanctity. Such customs and patterns can become the chains of the church, which need to be broken if we are ever to reflect the freedom of Christ. This does not mean that I am suggesting the destruction of everything old and familiar; but it is vital that we re-evaluate all our church life, and be able to justify what we do on the basis of its value in communicating Jesus Christ in present day culture.

Gifts of the King's children
One more plea: God has given you a gift, a ministry to the body of Christ, it may be obscure or obvious, whatever it is, have the courage to seek opportunities to exercise it.

It is not only our worship that needs revolutionary change. We must radicalise and strategise our outreach. For too long we have been happy to bumble along using the same methods as our fathers.

The revolution in communication technology must be matched by the church. There is no virtue in using outdated equipment or methods. At the local level evangelism must once again become the priority, the prime task of the church, and that means, of its individual members. When the church becomes primarily concerned with its own well-being and survival it ceases to be the Church of Jesus Christ the outgoing God, and becomes merely a cosy spiritual club. The favourite words of many church elders and officers 'we have never done it that way before' have been called the seven last words of a dying church. They could also be called the seven last words of a comatosed evangelist. All of us will need the courage to realise that we must do it – we must change the pattern.

The siege mentality has got to go: The time has come for us to go on the offensive. There is every indication that our culture is in the grip of an increasing spiritual hunger. Only a radical new strategy will meet it with the bread of life. The old patterns of evangelistic crusades will have to be dragged screaming into the twenty-first century. New methods will be needed, both at local church level and city-wide level. A new era in evangelism is coming. We have the opportunity of learning from the experience of the worldwide Church in South America, Korea and Africa. Out of their insights and our own long history of Christian witness God can forge a new weapon, a bright sword of battle with which to make inroads into Satan's territory: a new sharp scythe to reap vast fields which are already *'white and ready for harvest'*.

Witness of the King's children

Such evangelism will have to be rooted in the local church scene; founded on costly, loving relationships, inside and between local churches. The gospel is more important than the things which divide us; we dare not play games with the Lord's Church for the sake of our petty politics. May the Lord bring us to repentance, and then to bold action. Repentance in the Christian brings revival to the Church and that is the context in which the proclamation of the kingdom is truly effective. The Gospels tell us Jesus had compassion on the multitudes. Why not join him in that compassion, by giving yourself to praying that in the next few years hundreds of thousands of people will be brought into the kingdom of God by the Spirit of God? It will take costly personal witness, authoritative preaching of the gospel, and commitment to action to bring about the necessary changes. Hudson Taylor once wrote, 'Too often we attempt to work for God to the limit of our incompetence. We should work to the limits of his omnipotence.'

The kind of witness that confirms the claim that we have eternal life, is life that is irrepressibly full of joy and love, even in times of pain and distress. It has to last for ever, it could not die! Take that to work and people will have to take notice – which is what should happen if we are what we are meant to be. So many of us are strangely mealy-mouthed about Jesus Christ on the shop-floor, in the staff room or office, in the school or college. Faced with the opportunity to speak for Christ we mumble unconvincingly about going to church.

Lord have mercy upon us. Will you resolve today to surrender your working life to the living Christ? Will you become known not just as religious but as a disciple of Jesus Christ the Lord? As you liberate him to reign in the place where you work he will liberate you.

Holiness of the King's children

Holiness is recognising that God has called you to live for him in your unique situation: Butcher, bank clerk, secretary, dustman, toolmaker, computer operator, warehouseman, roadsweeper, nurse or tycoon, and yielding that to him so that he becomes the unseen 'boss'. Nobody else can live for Christ in the job that you do. That is your privilege and your pain, and it is different from any one else's. Just as every football match ever played is a different match though the rules are unchanged and unchangeable, so your working life is unique and unrepeatable. And as you commit it to Jesus it will also become inexplicable – apart from him, that is.

Holiness is not the absence of badness, not just a negative quality based on lots of prohibitions: Holiness is the positive presence of the life of Jesus. Your destiny is to so live with him that every moment becomes holy, lit up with him, shot through with heavenly meaning. You see, Jesus has set his name on you – his name is riding on you. He has chosen to continue his incarnation in you with all the risks that involves. As you allow the Lord to reign in you so he triumphs in you over the world, the flesh and the devil: you triumph and Satan cringes. If, however, you refuse to live in the kingdom of God by refusing to live in obedience to him then disaster is near, and in your fall the Lord's name is disgraced: Satan and his angels rejoice in triumph over the name of Jesus in you!

Enough to make us shudder – isn't it? No wonder C.T. Studd wrote:

> 'Let us not rust out. Let us not glide through the world and then slip quietly out without ever having blown the trumpet loud and long for our blessed redeemer. At the very least let us see to it that the Devil holds a

thanksgiving service in hell when he gets the news of
our departure from the field of battle!'

Amen!

Holiness is godliness with guts. It is something that God
has made available to all his people. So why are we still so
far short?

Dedicated, committed, consecrated, then re-dedicated,
re-committed and re-consecrated and even super-
committed, filled with the Spirit, refilled etc. What stops us
from possessing the land? What prevents us from moving in
the reality of the destiny formed for 'me' from eternity? It is
to our greatest problem, our deepest difficulty that we now
turn.

> 'Lord, I long to be a true disciple,
> Forgive me for the times I draw back in fear.
> Grant that the love I feel for you may grow to fill my
> whole being.
> Give me the courage to let go of all idols.
> By faith I abandon myself to the flow of your love.
> Amen.'

Chapter 7

Facing into the Sun

'Let's go at once and tell ...'

Evening at last. All day the sun had beaten down from a
cloudless sky. Later when the sun had gone and the rocks
lost their heat it would be cold. The four men in the shanty
that nestled close to the city wall pulled ragged coats about
them. Beggars people called them. Beggars they were,
though they had not always been so. One had been a
prosperous businessman, another a craftsman in metals,
the others labourers. Now they were united in two ghastly
fellowships, they were lepers, and they were starving.

Wordlessly they gathered together their meagre possessions: tried to make their tattered clothing a little present-
able. Talk was superfluous this evening. They had done all
that during the day and had reached an agreement that now
bound them. Tonight they were going to die; either that or
they would eat for the first time in days and they would live.
They wanted to live. They knew people said, 'Poor things,
they would be better off dead.' But they wanted to live, so
much so that this evening they were going to walk across
enemy lines and into the Syrian camp. The walls of the
besieged city shone in the dying rays of the evening sun as
the men took their last look. Inside, they knew, the skel-
eton prince Hunger ruled. Famine: gaunt, haggard women
had killed and eaten new-born babies, men bargained five
pieces of silver for half a litre of dove's dung.

It was time for them to leave.

As they approached the Syrian camp they were too nervous to notice the unusual quiet. This time in the evening should have been full of the noises of army camp life: evening trumpets calling, wood being collected and cut for the fires, cooking pots being re-stocked with ample food, sentries on guard duty exchanging good-humoured insults prior to the changing of duties.

The four reached the forward lines to find only an abandoned sentry post. As they penetrated the camp itself there was nobody to be seen anywhere. Horses tethered in picket lines whinnied in greeting but of the besieging Syrian army there was not a trace. Everywhere signs of panic, equipment abandoned, uniforms scattered and food, lots of lovely food.

Now the reality hit them. The Syrians had gone, without taking the food. They gorged until the hunger of months was satisfied with rich food and wine in plenty. Then they began systematically to loot the camp of valuables which they carefully stacked away in a secret cache.

It was while they were doing this that one of them suddenly remembered his family in the city: the city! The city where men and women waited for death to come on slow feet.

'We shouldn't be doing this! We have good news and we shouldn't keep it to ourselves. If we wait until morning to tell it, we are sure to be punished. Let's go at once and tell...'[1]

Precisely. Absolutely right!

The world is besieged by hellish powers, spiritually starving, haunted by guilt and desperately lonely. We gorge ourselves on the good news while we pay lip service to the idea of every Christian witnessing. But we don't **do** it.

Our great gospel

On two occasions Mark records Jesus as commanding sacrifice *'for my sake and the gospel's'*,[2] thus giving the **good news** the same priority as himself. Both Mark and Luke record Jesus as linking loyalty to himself with loyalty to his words: *'whoever is ashamed of me and of my words...'*[3]

What is this gospel that is so important to the Lord himself? First it is the good news of the kingdom of **Heaven** in which we are now beginning to live. It is a royal proclamation announcing and establishing the rule of heaven's King here on earth. Believing it humans may leave the kingdom of darkness which overshadows this world scene and become citizens of heaven while still living here on earth. It is marvellous news. Heaven is near and accessible. Long before death I can begin to live in heaven's reality.

Second, it is the kingdom of **God**: the wonderful news that God's authority is re-established on rebellious earth so that sin, death, misery and pain will one day be defeated. It is the announcement that we may come out from under the dread authority of Satan and enter the kingdom of God's dear son. It is the proclamation that a King reigns in majesty for ever, whose kingly power is founded on love, guaranteed by his battle-scarred body.

We have already seen that the prime aim of the gospel is not just the forgiveness of sins but the sovereignty of God in Christ. The end of the gospel, its ultimate objective, is the life of Christ – each Christian man and woman living as Jesus would have lived if he had been born in their time with their name. The gospel sets us free to shout to a world in despair, 'You can be what you are meant to be; your true destiny awaits you.' And the proclaiming is part of **our** true destiny!

Our strange silence

So many of our blessings are conditional on our courage in witnessing, our commitment to the gospel. The promise of the present companionship of Christ is made only to those who *'go into the whole world to preach the good news.'*[4] Our moment by moment experience and assurance of salvation depend on our speaking out the Lordship of Jesus.[5] Paul encouraged Timothy to pray for kings and governors and a *'quiet and peaceable life'*[6] only on the grounds that this was good for the spread of the gospel. If we are to enjoy the riches of our destiny we must become 'good newsers'.

Comments on religious matters thrown out apparently carelessly, in factory, school, college, office or shop, in fact, are often made as challenges. We must learn to pick up the gauntlet when it is thrown down or we disgrace our King. We are the message. We must **be** the gospel. In us the immeasurable greatness of his power is at work, the fountain of life, the abundance, dynamism and vibrancy of God. Through us the life of God bursts into the world and the world **must** feel the impact. The message matters. You and I are irreplaceable parts of it.

God's growing government
It was not only the gospel that Jesus placed on a par with himself: in Luke 18:29 he asked men to sacrifice property, relationships and family ties for the sake of the Kingdom, just as he had asked them to leave these things for His sake. He demanded a love for the kingdom so high that by comparison we would 'hate' parents, wife, brothers and sisters and our own life, and also renounce all our possessions. He presents us with an authority over us, so great that no other considerations matter. God's will alone counts and it is to the onward march of that will that you have pledged yourself in joining his kingdom.

C.S. Lewis once called God 'the Celestial Interferer' because God insists on disrupting all things in us that run counter to his will or that occupy a higher position in our affections than he does. This he does out of his love for us because we are committed to doing his will. So his government increases, and as it does, so does his peace in a process which should continue till the day we die. As we are continually learning his will in day by day encounter, so he continues the onward march of his kingdom by filling us human containers with the resurrection life of Christ. He does this for a purpose.

In us the God of heaven confronts the god of this world. Our commitment to a life of obedience is essential, if we are to be true citizens of the kingdom. I repeat, the King is supremely worthy of his authority for he has won it by winning the love of our hearts. Because we live under the authority of 'another King, Jesus' we are frontier people: we live at the frontier between heaven and earth. In fact, we are the frontier. The plan is that by prayer and spirit-inspired action we should extend that frontier to encompass others. Satan does not like that idea! Not surprisingly he tries to convince us that the job is too hard.

Weakness within

If he succeeds then we stop going out with any sense of triumph. No longer do we live with an eager offensive spirit scenting victory everywhere we go. Instead we live apathetically. Then the process often leads to retreat into the subculture of the church: where we may be soothed by comforting religious experience such as the apparent new strength of evangelicalism, by the blessings of the sacraments, or the comforts of the charismatic renewal. A deadly complacency results.

This is **not** the time to take things easy. An unseen battle rages about us. We are part of the great invasion force of the King of kings. The great missionary explorer David Livingstone said, 'I will place no value on anything I may have or possess except as it shall further the kingdom of God.' So let us be bold. We must live the life of the kingdom before this world and give it a glimpse of the coming reign of Christ.

We must do this for our own sake as well as the world's. Because a 'salvation' that is not an ongoing daily experience of Jesus changing me is a mere theological abstraction, a horrible deformity. It is not 'life' at all but a sub-life. It is terrifyingly possible for the **words** 'a personal relationship with Jesus Christ' to become a substitute for **living** that personal relationship with him. How do we escape? By living in daily obedience built on daily repentance. *'Repent for the kingdom of Heaven is at hand,'* Jesus said, and so it always is: the kingdom is near to a repentant person. As the kingdom extends the authority of Jesus in the soul so he or she begins to exert and extend the authority of the kingdom into the world around. Such a life is exciting, an adventure because it is involved daily in growing dependence on God.

The transforming vision

At the centre of the kingdom and the heart of the gospel is Jesus himself, for as we have seen, Christianity is not primarily a system of doctrine, philosophy, ethics, morals or ideals: Christianity is Jesus himself – a man to be loved, a master to be served, a King to be obeyed, a saviour to be received, God supreme in all things to be worshipped. Because of this a wrong vision of Jesus will be disastrous leading inevitably to a distorted version of Christian living. We must have a clear vision of that man: the best and bravest that ever was. To see him clearly by the Spirit is to be captivated and to love him. This is the love for which all our love relationships are practice runs. This is the real thing.

All love affairs transform the lover. This one changes us into the likeness of the beloved.

It is the very nature of lovers to gaze at each other for hours. In fact it is often hard to get them to do anything else! We have to learn to gaze on Christ with our inward eyes. We must learn the art of contemplation: the Holy Spirit in me meeting the Jesus in scripture. A vision of him is always a transforming vision. So the man or woman who has seen *'the light of the knowledge of the glory of God in the face of Jesus Christ'*, will find that glory settling in them, starting to raise them from one level of glory to another.

This is the basic principle of change in the Christian life: a vision of Jesus so real, so clear that it penetrates deep into us, changing us at the roots of our personality. But before this can happen we must believe that it is possible. This may be the greatest barrier to progress.

The tyranny of feelings

When all obvious sin is dealt with, a healthy diet of Bible reading, honesty in prayer and a rich pattern of fellowship have been created, we as Christian men and women will still stagnate, unless our deepest problem is solved. And the most fundamental problem of all humans facing their holy maker is the tyranny of feelings. When Satan seduced humanity away from the love relationship offered by the eternal God he so polluted the natural body, mind and emotions that it was no longer possible for us to know God as before. Worse, he removed for ever the possibility that had existed, that we should know God perfectly, thoroughly and in permanent experience flooding through every sense we possess.

He did this by encouraging Eve to a vague feeling of doubt about what God had said, which he then reinforced by telling her that God's motives were selfish. Though she clearly knew by past experience that God was good, Satan slowly, carefully, constructed a false picture of God and of her own feelings about him – these feelings became more real than her definite knowledge of God and his given word.

He then appealed to her appetite, her love of beauty and her intellectual vanity. In her response she elevated the entertained doubt and the aroused feelings of desire to a state of mastery over her. In his own decision to follow her lead Adam not only ratified her decision to trust present feeling over against the promise of an absent God, he probably added the twist of his own feelings for her. Created to be satisfied only by God himself, from that instant man and woman were subjected to a new inner tyranny, the ever present need to fulfil the desire of the moment. Since no one is ever in the position to satisfy every desire immediately, disappointment became the background to all of life. And because only the living God could fill the emptiness inside, the earthly kings and tyrants who were nearest to being able to satisfy every desire, experienced the greatest disillusion and emptiness. The feeling of disappointment, of inner sadness became common to all humans; in the self-indulgent usually becoming cynicism.

The lying vision

By constantly playing on our expectations and then dashing the hopes which had been aroused, Satan orchestrated in all mankind that profound doubt of promised good that sits deep in all of us. Our problem then, is that our enemy has painstakingly constructed in us a gaping void of mistrust. His whole strategy is directed towards making us feel that if God is real then he is mean, selfish, arbitrary and vindictive. He rarely denies God's power to help us or transform us; he does deny God's desire to do so. He presents to us a portrait of a cynical being playing games with human beings, his lips curled in amusement as he watches them struggle through the business of living, whose loving is a selfish manipulation of feelings for his own ends.

This picture of corruption finds a ready acceptance in us, for it accords with our own behaviour and is strengthened by our guilt – we know this is the sort of God we deserve. But the Bible cuts right across it all.

> '*O give thanks to the Lord, for he is good; for his steadfast love endures forever.*'[7]

Time and again the goodness, the unselfish loving of God is affirmed. Only the tendency to make a god in our own image, corrupt and selfish, prevents us from moving forward in faith. Often, those who say that they have intellectual problems believing in a good God are actually in the grip of the subjective reaction that **prefers** a wicked or amoral God, because that lays on them no moral imperative to change.

But we are not among their number if we know that God has spoken through his creation, through his written Word and through the eternal Word himself: the consistent message being 'The Lord is good. His loyal love goes on for ever.' This means that with confidence I can promise, 'God actually loves you; you, who you are, and He always has. He has only one plan. That is that you should walk in victory as Jesus did by the power of the Holy Spirit. He means you to be changed by his power into the image of Jesus Christ, so that people who meet you will be able to say, "Now I know what Jesus Christ is like. I have met him."'

Break the bondage

That is his destiny for you and nothing can stop it but your unbelief. You can decide to accept that God actually means this for **you**. He does. So now, once for all, break the yoke of tyranny! Smash the bondage of mere sentiment! Stand, a free man or woman, before the living God and commit yourself to the objective facts of his holy goodness, his selfless loving and the absolute reality of his revelation in Christ. Ignore your feelings. They are irrelevant in this instance.

You must give him the cold, clear, coolly calculated conviction of your mind, and commit yourself to that conviction – 'Jesus is **truth**. Jesus is God, God is love. These things I believe, **irrespective of my feelings**.' Once you settle yourself on that, a new reality begins.

Then you must give him the same calculated coolness in a total commitment of the will. 'Jesus Christ, you are Lord and God. You died for me because of your great love for me. My feelings are unreliable: I want you to know that irrespective of my feelings, I love you. Even if only ten per cent of me wants you I commit myself by voluntary act of the will to that ten per cent. I want you more than my own comfort. I love you now and will love you always.'

When you pray like this you are not only breaking free of the dominion of your feelings, you are taking the first steps in the process of bringing them into submission to Christ. You are taking those turbulent, rebellious, unreliable things inside you, dragging them by the scruff of the neck into **your** service, by subjecting them to your King. Now clearly, it is not simply a matter of saying words like those suggested above, but of involving **yourself** in such spoken commitments. And you must do this. The strength of your Christian life depends on your total commitment to the solid fact of the living God.

Your feelings must become your servants. Let them **follow** facts and they will trot obediently along behind them bringing life, joy and spontaneity. This pulsating, invigorating flow must never become the object of our believing, but it will be the outcome. So take charge! Remember David's orders to himself,

> *'Praise the Lord, **O my soul, and all that is within me** bless his holy name.'*

This does not mean we should be dishonest. Honesty has a vitally important place. The way you feel needs to be given to God in prayer. Faith demands only that this should no longer be the dominant factor in the relationship. You may tell the Father your heart is breaking, disaster threatens on every hand, and that you are unable to go on, provided that, even with tears streaming down your face you are also saying, 'But I trust you and I praise you, for you **are** great and you **love me**.' And that is love, real biblical love: the total dedication of the whole person to the good of another. It hurts! Of course it hurts: this is living out,

> *'Those who belong to Jesus Christ have crucified their human nature with all its passions and desires.'*[8]

This is dying with Christ; it may seem drastic, but it is better than living without him.

Moses discovered that.

The fiery vision
On the lower slopes of the mountains a bush suddenly burst into flame. Out here in the wild semi-desert near Mount Sinai such flash fires were not unusual in the terrifying heat of blazing mid-day sun. Moses continued on his way, the flock following as he looked for good grass. Again it caught his eye, still burning, which was odd. Such fires normally lasted only a few moments, and this one showed no sign of

dying down. Then he noticed something really strange; in spite of the roaring flames and white intensity of the fire the bush was not burning.

His curiosity drew him nearer, so that he could see there was no ash accumulating and no smoke rising through the still air. A tingling sense of something strange ran through him. Even the sheep seemed silent.

'Moses, Moses!' The voice was free, rich and full. It seemed to come from the heart of the flame.

'Here I am.'

Again the voice, glad, untamed and holy:

> *'Do not come any closer. Take off your sandals, because you are standing on holy ground. I am the God of your ancestors Abraham, Isaac and Jacob.'* [9]

A thrill of fear ran through Moses; now he knew why the flame had seemed to sear not only his eyes but his whole being. A swift movement brought his hood down low over his face – he was afraid to look any longer at the brightness.

That day Moses entered the service of the living God. Reluctant, afraid, unable to believe that he was actually chosen, wanted by the almighty, finally he fearfully agreed to enter upon his destiny. More unprepossessing material and a less auspicious start could hardly be imagined for Moses, the mighty deliverer, the great leader. He was to become a man of epic proportions. And the vision at the bush became the central passion of his life: the fear never left him, but he had seen something near Sinai that he loved. Years later it drew him back to Sinai with one aim, to see the face of God. Trembling with fear he walked up the mountain to see God face to face. When he finally came down the experience had transformed him, his face shone. For the radiation of God's holiness had poured into him: living purity, the intensity of eternal truth and the torrent of love had taken him to the limit of human capacity. God had answered his prayer and revealed himself to him as never to any man before or since.

> *'There has never been a prophet in Israel like Moses: the Lord spoke with him face to face.'*[10]

So the historian of Israel wrote after his death. But we live in the age of the new covenant. This is our privilege, for the Spirit is given to us for just this purpose, to lead us into all truth: into the refining fire that burns in the heart of God most high: and thus to be radiant with his glory upon us.

The fear we must confront
So what holds us back when we know that the real purpose of our existence, our destiny, is only to be found in him?

It is our low threshold of pain. In the western world self-indulgence has produced a soft, undisciplined generation, unused to discomfort of any kind, physical, mental or moral. Knowing God is painful. The problem is his holiness – his total purity and love: love which cares too much for our good ever to purchase our goodwill with gifts and bribes. Confronted with a love like his – an absolute commitment to ultimate good, to the happiness that can only derive from holiness – we are bound to feel discomfort. In fact we will feel pain. His holiness confronts my sin. His perfection confronts my imperfection. At every turn this hurts and always will. So we fear to come near to God.

One of the marks of holiness is, therefore, the ability to endure pain, the pain of his probing love as it goes on digging deeper into 'me' determined to cut out every last root and tendril of sin.

Few things that happen in the human body provide a better picture of sin than cancer, an active malignant growth consuming life from the body, often seeding other growths all over the body. Compare sin to cancer, and new birth is the moment when the main growth is cut out. The process of sanctification is allowing God's scalpel to do what a human surgeon cannot do; that is, to cut deeper and deeper into us, following the roots and tendrils along their winding courses into the very foundations of our conscious and subconscious beings. When our commitment is to him, the courses thus cleared continue to be clear and available to the river of life – the Holy Spirit. And the Holy Spirit is not given to us for our private enjoyment, but to drive us out from ourselves in two directions: into the world and up into our Father, but always away from ourselves.

So the world's torment will meet with God's redemptive pain; there will be a cross in us, in me.

The pain we must accept

If we are to be Christians living in the power of the Spirit of God then we must be Christians who are prepared to live under the constant pain resulting from continual confrontation with the holiness of God. But, once its essential nature is realised and accepted, this pain is a happy pain – a blissful, sweet pain as daily he drives deeper into 'me'. And since it is the route by which the river of the water of life flows through us the pain becomes part of the joy of victory.

Right here is the problem for western man in the late twentieth century. Such phrases as 'I die daily' and 'I have been crucified with Christ' have become poetic exaggeration rather than a literal description of a real and current experience. Or, worse, they have become the kind of language that one expects of a Premier League Christian like a St Paul or perhaps a missionary, but not the present experience of the 'ordinary Christian' still in the 'Sunday League'.

This double standard is dangerous because it enables us to live consistently below New Testament requirements without ever feeling guilty about it. 'After all no one expects the same standard of football from non-league clubs as from the Premier League giants. So why should we feel bad about our low standard of Christian achievement? All right for St Paul to talk about laying down one's life for the brethren but obviously impractical; fine for a first century evangelist with nothing to lose, but not so good for urban and suburban man with all his commitments and conveniences. It's nice to be idealistic, but we have got to be down-to- earth.' Worse still, this attitude can spill over onto Jesus himself. 'All right for him to talk about loving God with all the heart, soul, mind and strength: after all, he was perfect. Nobody else is...'

The goal we should aim at

We find it so easy to forget his command to us, 'Be perfect.' But in addition to the commandment, we have the promise of power, not only the map with destination clearly marked we have also the fuel to get there. The Spirit of God really can take an ordinary man or woman right into the purifying furnace of the heart of God; and he will do it for you and me if we will let him.

God's purpose in revealing his holiness to us is not to condemn us but to transform us, to change us from the inside by a constant process of cleansing, purifying and filling us. For this, all he needs from us is a continual response of repentance: moment by moment agreeing with God that he is right and we are wrong; daily exposing to the Father all we have done including even the hard-heartedness that feels no sorrow or regret for sin. That also is sin and it will begin to die as we continually expose it to the radiance of God's holiness. Strangely our reaction when we truly encounter that is usually one of surprise. We expect it to condemn us, instead it seems to challenge and encourage. We expect it to reject us, but it accepts us. Its gentleness woos us rather than threatens. Surrendering to its imperative we move into greater and greater freedom as the Maker increasingly releases us into what we were meant to be.

As a result of this ongoing surrender, as we hold ourselves before him always repentant, always open, we live in the now with God who himself is always in the 'now'. We begin sharing that state of eternity known as everlasting life. At last!

The same abiding love for the Father that motivated Jesus will begin to motivate us. We will start to do the will of the Father naturally, because we want to. This is the same day-to-day choice as he made: *'I do always those things I see the Father doing.'* For his sake committed to loving our neighbour, we can find the power to endure in the pain of sacrificial caring, because it is the Father's love that is now available through us. This is the service that is perfect freedom: the joyous liberation of finally finding out what we are really meant to be. 'Love God and do as you like.'

Practical pointers:

1. Practise positive prayer. Don't let your prayer be dominated either by a recitation of all your troubles or by a long 'shopping list'. Tell God how great he is. Affirm what you know of his goodness and love. **Practise** telling him that you love him and trust him.
2. Part of the confrontation with him is the lives of other Christians. Look for someone who **knows** God better than you do. (Not about him, that is not necessarily the same.) Be prepared to commit yourself to that person for a time to learn what they have learnt of him. The revelation coming through them will teach you the truth of God's transforming power.
3. Look for the present tense in Scripture. For example, after building a historical foundation Paul speaks of present experience in Romans chapters 5 and 8. Enter that reality. God is always present tense.

This prayer may help you express your desire to be holy.

Lord you are great, the Maker of all things.
Forgive me that I so often turn from you, when I long to move towards you.
Take charge of my emotions.
Reign over them, that they may become a pathway for your Spirit.
Make me holy, that I may be happy.
Amen.

Chapter 8

Facts are Better than Dreams

'... although impatient for the morning I slept soundly and had no need of cheering dreams. Facts are better than dreams.'[1]

The Bible – truth is not boring

The Bible. The most important and fascinating book the world has ever seen. Not so much a book – more a library of life. It is a collection of books encompassing a bigger vision of each person and their place in the whole creation than anyone ever dreamed of. Starting with the making of the universe it ends with its destruction and remaking. Not just earthbound in its understanding, it rises even above the galaxies and places humanity in a cosmic context.

The first historical books present a picture of human lives intertwined with great events on a scale that dwarfs *War and Peace*. The cast list of characters includes heroes, villains, kings, shepherds, farmers, murderers, thieves, rapists, saints, prophets, priests, lovers and a talking donkey. Later the history weaves its pattern around two kingdoms, one with its long dynasty from a single family and the other featuring a series of bloody coups that make our own history look positively anaemic. Successive invasions by ruthless armies of conquest from the emerging empires to the east and south, end in the collapse first of one and finally the other kingdom. Then follows the agony of a nation in chains as the whole Jewish people are dragged into exile. Through it all is shown the never-ending love of God to whom they pledged themselves in covenant relationship, only to break the covenant over and over again. His loyal love for the nation of Israel and Judah is a constant song of heartbreak. The repeated pattern of rebellion makes it necessary for the loving Father of Israel to act in anger: discipline and chastisement are the pain-filled obligations of parental love. And while all this is happening fascinating characters emerge for a moment and then disappear again: Benaiah went down into a pit on a snowy day – the Bible doesn't say why – but while he was there he killed a lion; Jael, who gave a bottle of milk to the wicked tyrant Sisera and then banged a tent peg into his head while he slept!

Boring? How could anyone say it was boring? Vast in its scope and often gruesome in its factual depiction of human wickedness, it may be difficult in places but boring – never! And it is all true.

The Bible – real relationships with a real God
It is what Francis Schaeffer calls true truth because it really happened. It is a record of the actions of the living God in relationship with human beings, the story of his long battle with Satan to try to prevent him from dragging the millions on earth into hellish misery and emptiness. God has acted in human history and people have either joined with him or fought against him.

Out of the experience of those who committed themselves to him came poetry and drama which are often sublime in their imagery. They present a unique collection of personal experiences plumbing the depths of human misery, rising through great happiness to the uttermost edges of God-given bliss. Then come the books of history, prophecy and ancient lament, that are known as the prophets. Full of passion, fire and burning calls for revolutionary change in society, these books have stimulated, excited and scared the people of God through the centuries. They are still frighteningly relevant.

The prophets' promise that God will come to his people is thrillingly vindicated in the Gospels in the coming of Jesus and the gift of the Holy Spirit. That invasion of life and joy ushers in the age of the Church, and within this growing community letters are exchanged that still today sparkle with bubbling life. The book is capped by an amazing piece of literature called Revelation. Often discredited by the idiocy of Christendom's fringe loonies, it is the most marvellous epic romance in the world. It tells the story of the bride-to-be held in terrible captivity by a wicked dragon for years of torment. Tortured, wounded, often appearing to be near to death, she holds on in hope, believing that one day the promised prince will come. Then he does come, riding a white horse, a conqueror who kills the dragon, rescues her and carries her off to live with him for ever. Never were the words truer, 'And they all lived happily ever after.'

That part is yet to be. But, have no doubt, it will happen, for the Bible is utterly reliable. Facts, facts, facts from beginning to end. Its performance record so far is excellent.

The Bible – reliable truth

'Facts are better than dreams.' When Churchill wrote that, he was speaking as a warrior faced with the task of winning a war. Whatever you may think of him personally, his assessment of the position was correct. In such a situation a man or woman needs facts. Solid facts. And the Bible is solidly factual, stubbornly reliable, historically, archaeologically and scientifically. It is also reassuringly human.

I once did a survey of people's attitude to Jesus and the church. Equipped with BBC-type tape recorder slung over my shoulder and microphone to thrust between people's teeth, I asked first, 'What do you think of the church?' Some of the replies were unprintable, others typical.

One rather generously proportioned, breathy lady in her fifties beamed at the question. Her wide brimmed hat and impeccable clothes oozed prosperity.

'The church? Wonderful, wonderful.'

'Thank you. Would you mind telling me how often you go to church?'

'Oh, every week. Would never miss it.'

'I see. What do you think of Jesus?' Her smile vanished.

'Jesus? Oh, nothing at all. He's nothing to do with it. Some form of Higher Thought. That's what matters.'

I think that she would not really have approved of the Bible's bluntness about such matters as King Saul entering a cave to relieve himself or the promise of the Rabshakeh to the besieged population of Samaria that they would be reduced to eating their own dung? Such things hardly come under the heading of Higher Thought! But the Bible is embarrassingly frank – to prissy twentieth-century ears – about basic biology, precisely because it is completely honest about our humanity and our fallenness. From beginning to end it is inspired by the Spirit of God who can never lie. This makes it impossible for the writers ever to put a gloss on any character, to dress him up! So all the characters are there 'warts and all'. And because it never tries to do that to people, it never has to 'improve on' or embroider events in which people are involved. It is historically reliable because the Spirit of God would not allow anyone to alter the record of history. The New Testament is already recognised by many historians as being the most reliable historical document of its time. And the Old Testament, once so besieged by critics, is steadily being vindicated as archaeology produces more and more evidence to confirm its record. It is rather fun to see the critics retreat in confusion!

The Bible – inconvenient truth
Of course, some philosophers and theologians still attack the biblical story but they tend to do so more on philosophical grounds. Since much modern philosophy is directed largely by subjective preference, not facts, there is no refuting such views. One suspects they prefer it that way.[2]

If I said that the Bible was as solidly true as granite, I would be doing it less than justice. I have never yet heard of a piece of granite that grew larger when pieces were chipped off – but the Bible has a habit of growing in stature and circulation when it is attacked.

Sometimes Christians are accused of wishful thinking when it comes to the authority of the Bible. In my case I must confess this is true. I have often wished that it were **not** true; for moral, or rather immoral reasons! But I am glad that this book boldly continues to condemn my behaviour until I return in honest confession to the feet of Jesus Christ and there find the release of forgiveness, and power to live right.

The spirit of our age is a very proud one – it is part of our cultural thinking that we are more advanced than the people of previous centuries, and therefore the further back in history, the more primitive people were. Such arrogance. Try telling that to Pythagoras!

So there are people, and you may be one, who say that while they can accept Jesus as real and truly the son of God they cannot accept the Old Testament. When asked why the apostles under the influence of the Holy Spirit believed it to be true, they say they were 'prisoners of their culture'. They will even say that Jesus only accepted the Old Testament because 'he was a man of his time, a prisoner of his culture'. This is such nonsense. If ever a man was free, really free, Jesus was that man; never was a man less a prisoner of his time or a mere product of his environment. He was intellectually, emotionally and physically a free man under the Father God's guidance. We are the real prisoners when we cannot break free of the arrogance of this age and accept the timelessness of truth. The Bible is true.

The Bible – permanent truth

Another strand of the spirit of our time is concerned to destroy any idea of the permanence of truth, and to replace it by a disposable throwaway faith which happens to be 'true for me at this moment'. The poet Steve Turner wrote a brilliantly biting parody of this attitude and called it 'Creed'. Part of it goes:

'I believe that each man must find the truth that is right
for him.

Reality will adapt accordingly. The universe will read-
just.

History will alter.

I believe that there is no absolute truth excepting the
truth that there is no absolute truth.'[3]

The Christian belief of some people is just a religious
version of that. A university chaplain once told me that it
was not necessary to believe anything at all: 'There is no
minimum of faith necessary to be a Christian.' Such people
are well-meaning robbers of the faith. They destroy the
great building of Christian belief, then vandalise the foundations and all in the name of a God of love, whose actual
character and person become vaguer and emptier the
longer one looks. They think they are helping, but in fact
they rob people of God-given certainty.

In their hands the church becomes a dream factory dominated by a 'spirituality' related more to paganism than the
outpoured spirit of Christ. Elitism is inevitable. The church
of Jesus the Christ who valued all kinds of people becomes
the dominion of the 'naturally spiritual', the esoteric, the
ones with secret knowledge.

Thank God for the facts! Because everybody, whether
they are naturally religious or not, may trust the written
Word of God and by doing so meet Jesus the eternal
personal Word of God. The everliving God has given us his
message and by his written promises a man may begin
acquaintance with him. For that is the whole purpose of the
Bible. God-breathed and infallible, it calls us to the knowing of the Father-Maker, and provides all the information
we need, pointing without fail to him. But this does not
mean that knowing the Bible is the same as knowing God.
There are some people for whom the written Word has
become more important than Jesus, the Word himself. The
map has become more important than the route and the
destination. This is a terrible perversion of truth and is

really idolatry. In fact, it might best be called bibliolatry. Because of its very character this temptation can only come to religious people of orthodox, usually Protestant, faith.

The Bible – the way to the Way
The Pharisees were orthodox. In all things they upheld a high view of their Jewish Bible believing it to be inspired by God and infallible. Yet Jesus said to them,

> *'You search the scriptures, because you think that in them you have eternal life; and it is they that bear witness to me; yet you refuse to come to me that you may have life.'*[4]

The scriptures are meant to lead us to him and when they do not, it is tragic. To read the written words of God and not, at the same time to hear the voice of God inwardly, is an awful denial of the function and reality of both.

For this is where the quest begins. The search to know God as no one else ever did commences right here before the open pages of the Bible. It is such a rich and varied book that through it God can speak to you as he never quite spoke to anyone. This is where his unique revelation of himself to you starts. It is the only sure way by which you can make your way into his heart, for here in these pages he has bared his heart:

> *'My anguish, my anguish! I writhe in pain!*
> *Oh, the walls of my heart!*
> *My heart is beating wildly;*
> *I cannot keep silent;*
> *for I hear the sound of the trumpet, the alarm of war.'*[5]

That is the pain of a loving Father who sees his rebellious children plunging headlong into all the misery of war. Now God's purpose in giving such words is to lead you through those words to him. The words are a gateway into him. The one condition is that you must recognise that only God can

tell you the truth about himself. Therefore if you are to
know him, even through the Bible, you must claim his help,
otherwise it will be a dead book to you. You need the Spirit
of God to lead you.

The Bible – the word of the Word

Earlier in this book we talked about Jesus and his title the
Word of God. Sometimes the Bible is also called the Word of
God; that is the revelation of God written, just as Jesus is the
revelation of God in the definitive human being. The written
Word comes to us, by the Holy Spirit of God, from the
eternal Word. So it is the word of the Word of God. Jesus
Christ is revealed and expressed in every part of the Bible.
The eternal Word, Jesus himself, waits to meet you in
different ways on every page. The truth of the living God.

And here is where we plunge back into the mainstream
of our theme. You are unique, different from anyone else
ever born. When God spoke out in creative power the word
that became you, he said something he had never said
before and will never say again. Therefore when the message of the Bible meets the message you are, an entirely
new revelation of God's character is unveiled. God has
things to say to you through the Bible that he can never say
to anyone else – for if he did they would never hear them in
quite the same way. He is the living God, limitless in his
personality and creation: he has so much to say and only
eternity in which to say it! We can all know the broad
outlines of his character – the soaring, blazing mountain
peaks of his holiness, the warm spice-scented valleys of his
love, the ocean-dark depths of his humility: But the intricate facets of his person as Father and lover you alone and I
alone can know, only as we know him, one to one. The holy
ground on which we stand as we do this – the infallible rock
of God's book.

Approach it with thought

Now this does not mean that we regard the Bible with
superstitious awe, never daring to think about it. We are to

use our brains to try to understand and apply its teaching. *'We are to handle it like skilled workmen knowing how its parts fit.'*[6] But we are never to elevate reason above the Bible. If something is true but beyond our understanding that does not mean it is untrue! It simply means we do not yet have the insight to grasp it. Spiritual perception is something that grows within us as we are exposed to the voice of God – and the surest way to hear that voice is through a steady programme of Bible reading, while maintaining an attitude of openness to the Holy Spirit. The Bible is spiritual food. Therefore every time we open the Bible we should expect God to feed the life of Christ into us, expect to receive a revelation of Jesus.

Remember it is possible for brilliant theologians to study the Bible for years and never see Christ as who he is – the eternal God in flesh. Sometimes ministers of the Church are trained out of it, and it takes years to get back to the simplicity of meeting Jesus in the written Word. So when we read the Bible we should do so, not primarily to formulate doctrine but to know God in Christ. Our theology should spring out of this interaction – faith and reason meeting revelation.

You see, Jesus Christ is the key to the Bible. Once we have received him as King and as the one who died for us, we begin to know him and he begins to unlock the mysteries of the book. So we can confidently expect him to show us something each day **provided we ask him**.

Approach it with prayer
'Jesus Christ, you are the Word, the message of God. As I read this book give me your Spirit and show yourself to me, I want to know you. As I get to know you, make the Father real to me so that I will know him and begin to live like his child.'

Approach the Bible with that kind of prayer on your lips and I promise you God will speak to you, though not always in the same way. It varies tremendously in its texture and make-up. As I have already said, it is spiritual food, but food comes in many forms.

Occasionally I take my wife out to a restaurant for a beautifully prepared and presented meal. We really enjoy these occasions but there are times when a poached egg on toast or 'mince' with mashed potatoes and peas can taste like food of the gods. Great thick chocolate eclairs oozing dairy cream; crusty wholemeal rolls filled with fresh lettuce, tomatoes and a slice of ham, or simply a piece of crusty bread torn from a fresh loaf, a bowl of porridge; all of it is food. All of it gives nourishment. Some kinds of food are more exciting than others – they all have their place in a healthy diet. Sometimes Bible reading is solid, stodgy like a bowl of porridge; still like porridge it is food and is building you up, though you may not know it. For the living Christ is in it all. And that is why every Christian should read the whole Bible. The whole Bible? Yes, but not all at once, there are ways. We shall look at them later.

The old Anglican Prayer Book calls the communion service 'a holy mystery' – saying that Jesus is present in a spiritual and heavenly way in the bread and wine. In the same way Jesus is present in the Bible, mystically, spiritually, truly there. It is an ordinary book made of ordinary paper and ink but when you open its pages to seek him he pours upon you the power of his presence, the rich torrent of his life streams out to meet you and fill you. The reality expressed in words on paper is conveyed by the Holy Spirit from behind the words into you. You are feeding on the living God. And just as Jesus promised, this feeding on him, this recognition, that here is the one whose body was broken for me, here is the one whose blood was spilt for me, brings life! For the life of the loving God is in his love letter to you, and when your ears are spiritually open you hear him saying, 'I love you, I love you and I love you.'

Set within the context of this kind of relationship the voice of God guiding you is no longer the 'hit and miss' business it so often seems to be. The key to the problem of guidance is first knowing the sound of God's voice, so that before any other factors enter, you clearly know what he has said. Reading the Bible attunes your spiritual ear to the 'sound' of his call.

Approach it with sense

'OK so it's great. I tried to read the whole Bible and got stuck halfway through Exodus. All those curtains, rods and rings, fine-twined linen, badger skins and tent pegs! I couldn't keep going. It was so boring! What does all that have to do with Jesus?' The answer to that question is, 'Right now, not very much. Before you can make that sort of connection, you have to know a lot more about Jesus.'

I want to be very practical at this point and try to suggest ways in which the many people who know they ought to read their Bibles but never do it, may begin. First, understand that for the vast majority of people, beginning at Genesis and reading through to Revelation is just not possible. Jesus is the key to the whole book so a basic knowledge of the New Testament, by which I mean a reading knowledge, will help to light up the Old Testament. Of all the ways of studying the Bible the most important is simply reading it; because reading is the basis for all other methods of study.

So how do you start?

If you have had trouble with Bible reading before, you would probably find it helpful to buy a new one, one of the modern versions. Go to a good bookshop and ask to see:

New Revised Standard Version
Good News Bible
New International Version
Living Bible
New Jerusalem Bible
(There are several other versions available)

Read a few sample paragraphs from different parts of each version, then decide which will suit you. For your start you may prefer to buy only a New Testament or even just one gospel. The Good News gospels are particularly suitable for beginning serious Bible reading. Having chosen your Bible or New Testament, you are ready to start. A quiet place; a good chair; a prayer that says 'Jesus, this is your book. By your Spirit show me yourself. I am open to you,' and you are ready to start.

So where do you start?

Approach it with Jesus

Start with Jesus. Start with one Gospel.

Which one? Again, you look and choose.

Mark is the shortest and the fastest moving, probably dictated by Peter; this is the action gospel showing us Jesus the Servant of God and men. Luke is the longest and the most flowing narrative; probably the best picture of Jesus the man. Matthew, slightly shorter than Luke, was written to show Jesus as the promised King of the Jews; many links with the Old Testament. John, written some years after the others to paint a portrait of the man who was God; it is the inside story of his teaching and training of the disciples.

Whichever one you choose, read it as fast as you can – most of us can easily read a few chapters a day if we try. While you read, carry on praying 'Jesus make yourself real to me.' Read that gospel three or four times, and where God speaks to you through it, mark the page with a coloured pencil or pen. Don't be afraid to make notes all over it if they help. Just make it **your** Bible.

Then start on the other Gospels by reading all four – Matthew through to John three or four times. By now you will be really getting to know the God-man Jesus. So when you reach the end of John on the third or fourth occasion keep going straight on to the end of Revelation. If you hit problems, make a separate note so that you can ask someone else about them, then carry on reading. Above all, remember this book is a love letter from the Father-Maker to you – through it he will speak to you as his son/daughter, and he will use it to speak as he never quite spoke before. This is your destiny – don't forget it.

When you have read the New Testament three or four times you will be ready to tackle the whole of the Old Testament!

It may be helpful to remember that roughly one half of the Old Testament is taken up by the historical books Genesis to Esther. The other half is made up by poetical books Job to Song of Solomon and the prophets Isaiah to Malachi. You may like to begin at Genesis and Job and thus change the mood day by day. By the way, whatever you do, do not drop the reading of the New Testament; carry on getting to know Jesus and he will continue to lead you. When you feel discouraged remember that just three chapters a day will take you through the Bible in one year!

Approach it in freedom
If that makes you feel worse then simply relax, stop worrying and keep on reading at the rate that suits you; whatever you do, keep on reading and receiving the Holy Spirit so that he can take the scriptures and out of them make Jesus real to you in a new and never-to-be-repeated way. Alternatively, try the various 'One Year Bibles'.

Once, when some intellectual characters asked him a foolish question Jesus replied,

> *'How wrong you are. It is because you don't know the scriptures or God's power.'*[7]

Without knowing the Bible we all run the risk of becoming as silly as they were.

Worse, without knowing the Bible you will find it almost impossible to place your feet on the path of your destiny. For the God who wants to reveal himself to you, as never to any other human being, waits to begin within the pages of that book. His terrifying, unending love for you, the reason for your living, the fulfilment of all you are.

So what are you waiting for? Boldly go...!

Jesus, you are the Word of God.
Open my eyes to see you in the Bible.
By your Spirit be real to me.
Never let me be ignorant of the scriptures
or of God's power.
Thank you for helping me.
Amen.

The Word of God has another title: the sword of the Spirit. We need such a weapon because of the frighteningly real battle in which we are involved. Locked in combat in a heavenly war we must learn to use heavenly weapons. So now we turn to the subject of prayer, the Christian's guided missile.

Chapter 9

The Inter-Cosmic Ballistic Missile

'Now war arose in heaven ... And the great dragon was thrown down, that ancient serpent, who is called the Devil and Satan, the deceiver of the whole world – he was thrown down...'[1]

Prayer is vital

All around the battle rages and of its elements, prayer is probably the least understood. It is possible that, in the minds of many people, the two words 'prayer meeting' constitute the most boring phrase ever invented. Yet for those who have learned anything at all about it, real prayer is the most exciting activity the world has ever known, because prayer is the way in which you and I actually take part in the invisible realities of the heavenly realm – and our contribution is vital to the outcome of the hidden battle. You have, I have, a key part to play.

The titanic struggle between the God of heaven and the King of darkness, is even now raging unseen across the face of the globe; in it our prayers play the decisive part. The victory of Golgotha, when Jesus, the son of man in ordinary flesh and blood, confronted the full power of Satan and defeated it, was the climax not the end. To his Bride, the Church, is given the privilege of encompassing the final downfall of Satan. This she does by the power of God who has given his authority to her. Even before the coming of Christ men knew what it was to see miracles by prayer...

121

Prayer is warfare

It was becoming obvious that some malicious will was at work within the people of Israel.[2] There was continual grumbling, and quarrels seemed to break out with little reason. Few of them understood why they must journey through the stark barrenness of the wilderness to the holy mountain. Horeb some called it – Mount Sinai which stood in an area of jumbled rocky peaks in the south of the wilderness of Paran. Moses knew only too well that someone was opposing the people of Yahweh in their march southwards to meet with their God at Sinai. If confirmation were needed it was there in the solid shape of the Amalekite army.

It was clear that, hearing of Israel's escape from Egypt and the call to return to the land of promise, and fearing that Israel would attack them on the way through to Canaan, the Amalekites had mobilised their army to meet and defeat the nation far south and west of their own borders. Today the decisive battle would be fought. In the quiet darkness just before dawn Moses and some attendants had climbed up the highest hill in the area so that the whole valley lay before them. As the sun tipped over the horizon the first rays touched the summit of holy Sinai far to the south and Moses' pulse quickened. Win this battle and the way would be open. There the holy presence waited for him. He turned back to look at the valley below, still in darkness.

He knew Joshua had roused the men early and was even now deploying his forces for assault on the Amalekite positions. The sun rose swiftly, spilling light into the valley. Standing on the edge of the hill so that his silhouette could be clearly seen he raised his hand, in it the rod of God: symbol of holy authority. Suddenly the stillness was shattered by the brazen blare of trumpets. Attack!

The Israeli signal was answered by Amalekite buglers: 'To Arms!' For the inexperienced soldiers of Israel who now faced the accomplished Amalekite army this was to be a make or break day. If they were defeated here in their first battle, they might never survive as a nation.

And Moses knew it.

Prayer is hard work

And he knew too that their real hope was not in the new young recruits who even now were advancing over the ground slippery with blood, hideous with severed limbs and spattered brains. Their hope was in the authority of God. Sweat streamed down his aching arm as he continued to hold up the rod. Whenever he tried to rest his arms by dropping them the battle started to go against Israel. He knew he must stand with hands raised in triumph over the battle until it was won. Both his arms began to tremble with exhaustion. Still the battle raged on. Aaron and Hur who had climbed up with him realised they must do something to help Moses go on with his proclamation of God's power. Together they strained to lift a huge stone into position behind Moses so that he could sit; then they took one arm each and held them – held the hands up in the position of authority and triumph. The Amalekites were mown down, their remnants broke and fled, the way was open.

Before they left the area Moses erected an altar and called it 'The Banner of the Lord'. He said that he had had 'a hand on the banner of the Lord'. What a marvellous description of prayer: putting a hand on the banner – sign of royal presence and power – of the Lord. But remember this kind of prayer had its roots in Moses' previous acquaintance with God. At the burning bush he had met him and begun there a conversation that continued until the day he died. Moses knew God as no man ever did.

Prayer is intimacy with God

But then, that is your calling – ever since the dawn of the church age with the coming of the Holy Spirit, it has been possible for all who trust in Christ to know the Father with the same intimacy as Moses. And that means to know him as no one else ever did: taking your own special individual nature to him and find its meaning in knowing him. All of us establish our identity by meeting others – in relationship with them we fix the shape and borders of our own personality. So the first function of prayer is to establish and enjoy the relationship with the Father. Remember where the Lord's Prayer begins: 'Our Father in heaven'. It begins with relationship. Your first object in praying must be to know him, and to let him know you. So prayer itself should never become a barrier between you and him.

Yet it often does become a barrier; some people feel they should only pray in a certain position or place, or at a certain special time of the day. Still more employ a special set of words for prayers and even a special tone of voice. Such things are barriers to relationship. God has called you to know him and to find out something in him that no one ever knew before. He is Father and understands you better than anyone. So relax. If you find it hard to pray sitting or kneeling then walk around the room or else the park. And tell him the truth, the utter truth about yourself. Use your normal language and bare to him your feelings; joy, grief, frustration, boredom anger. Even if you are angry with him, he is a very big Daddy – he can take it! As you open yourself to him you will find him beginning to fill up empty places in you, to heal ancient wounds and ease long established pain. The words God and Father will cease to be empty words, they will become a person known and beloved. And his constant outpouring of love to you will increasingly set you free to be who you are – for in his love you will come to know your real value.

From the moment of his meeting with God at the burning bush Moses was a man who was being changed. And it started when God said,

> 'Take your shoes off. You are standing on holy ground.'[3]

He was not so much saying Moses' shoes were defiling holy ground but saying 'no barriers between us'. The cost of real prayer is to walk with no shoes on God's road; sometimes a road strewn with thorns.

Prayer is transforming

As you are open to him in prayer he will change you. That is the second function of prayer; to transform people. Getting to know the God of heaven we are tinged by his radiance: the child begins to take on the family look, the likeness of the Father. So give him a chance. Spend time in his presence. In our tense activist world it requires time and practise to relax – but it is worth investing in knowing God. Learn just to be in his presence and to know his greatness as God all around you – the great calm stillness of his peace, the peace of God that beats all our understanding. In a crazy, tensed-up, frenetic world someone who knows the Father and has received his peace is rare and beautiful, like a shaft of sunshine on a day of clouds and drizzle.

As we have seen, this kind of transformation is your God-given right, for it is your destiny planned from before the world's making and bought at the cost of his life by Jesus Christ. And the Bible says you can be what you are meant to be, not only because of his sacrifice in history, but because of his constant work on your behalf now. It tells us that the man Jesus now stands before the judgement throne of God hearing and answering the accusations that Satan loves to bring against you. He is your representative before the Father. Every time Satan accuses you of sin Jesus reminds the holy God and Father that his death has covered your sin, just like a rich friend might cover the debts of a bankrupt. In addition he comes to you to reveal to you the character of the Father. That is the work of a priest – to plead for humans before God and to bring God's revelations to them.

Prayer is for all

In the old covenant, before Christ, men of a certain family were appointed as priests within Israel and they carried that privilege and dignity as long as they lived. Jesus' death and ascension changed all of that. The old barrier of the rebellion and fall was torn down and people could once more walk with God. Many times the Bible says all Christians are priests – there is no longer a special class. Now the

Church may ask some of us to bear that title, as a reminder of the function of all Christians, but we who are called priests are no longer the intermediaries by which others must contact God. Jesus the man is the only intermediary now needed. That is why you can truly know God the Father, because his son is constantly standing between you to introduce you to each other.

Once you have received the life of Jesus Christ the Son of God you also have become a child of God and an heir of God's kingdom. You are now a partner in the family business because you are part of the family. So the great High Priest Jesus Christ appoints you to join him in his priest-hood, to stand with him before the throne of God, bearing the needs and torment of a world in chains. This is the third function of prayer. And it is no good saying this is only for special people because he will simply reply that you are special. The high calling is yours. It is your destiny and your meaning.

Prayer touches others
There are certain people who are closer to you than they are to any other Christian; your wife, children, husband, girl-friend, boy-friend, fiancée, neighbours and workmates. The thrilling responsibility of priesthood is yours. Job had seven sons and three daughters. He was a rich man and they enjoyed a full life including many parties which by eastern custom could last for days. Job used to get up early on the morning after each party and pray that God would forgive each of his children for any foolish or unintentional sin. He knew that being a father and head of the family meant acting as a priest to each member of the family.

You have the right to pray for others that God's will shall be done in their lives. This is your privilege and part of the reason God made you. He knew that through your prayers he could touch certain people in power, that he could reach no other way. What a marvellous thing, to be part of God's unfolding will in someone else's life. All Christians have this power. Because we are humans, heirs of Adam, we have authority in heaven itself.

So in praying, we bring together earth and the power of **heaven**. We bring down heaven's authority into earth. This is our mission; to link a loving all-sufficient God and the weak of the earth. We stand for them before him. God hears us and loves to answer our prayers when they are his own Spirit-breathed response to a situation.

Prayer opens the door to healing
The heat in the little house near the sea was almost unbearable. People from every little village of Galilee were crowding in to listen to the teacher. The best seats had been taken by rows of local ministers and Bible students who sat listening hour after hour, occasionally smiling and at other times muttering to each other, their brows knit in disapproval.

For some time a steady stream of sick and injured people had been brought in for healing and there had been many miracles. But now the crush within the small building made it impossible to get through. The crowd filled the grounds of the house and the street outside.

Paralysed, he lay on his stretcher and listened to the arguments as his friends tried to force a way through the solid mass. It was no good. Privately he felt sure that this also was part of his judgement, he had sinned enough. God knew he deserved his punishment, he certainly did not deserve to be healed; it was hopeless. His friends seemed to agree: they gave up trying to get in and started to go back down the street. The stretcher rocked uneasily as they pushed against the flow of the crowd.

Suddenly it was quiet and raising his head he could see they were out of the crowd moving down a narrow side street. Then he understood. They were going to approach the house from a different direction. Finally they were close to the house and the stretcher was lowered to the ground. When they had explained the plan he was sure they were crazy! Surely the teacher would not thank them for dropping in on him like this! What marvellous mates they were.

Riding their shoulders up the steps at the side of the house was worrying enough, let alone listening to them breaking up the tiles and twigs of the roof. But swaying uneasily over the heads of the crowd as they lowered the stretcher on ropes into the room was an experience he would never forget. Then the teacher was there looking at him. He felt that his sins showed as clearly as if they were scrawled in scarlet letters on his face. Utter hopelessness gripped him as he remembered his guilt. When he raised his eyes again the teacher was not looking at him, but at the grinning faces peering through the hole in the roof. 'You can do it, Master,' one of them said. 'Nobody knows what's wrong with him but you can heal him,' said another.

Again the teacher looked down. His eyes were piercing . . . painfilled.

'Your sins are forgiven.'

There was a moment of silence then the babble of argument and protest broke out; no matter. He knew, somehow in those seconds the teacher had taken the guilt from him. It had cost him, too, he could see that. There was an argument still going on – then the teacher looked at him again.

'I say to you, get up. Pick up your stretcher and go home.'

He did it. Simple as that. Did it, and went home singing 'Glory to God.'

Jesus was able to do that because he saw 'their' faith – the faith of the man's friends. They did not know it, but their action was a priestly one – costly in time and effort and demanding on their commitment. They had brought a weak, guilty, paralysed man into the presence of the Christ.

Prayer touches the invisible
And this is our privilege too. In prayer we actually touch the hidden realities – we deal in issues more solid and real than even the physical pains. We touch eternal immensities. If only we would grasp the enormous possibilities of these things then the prayer life of the church would be

transformed overnight. Ordinary Christians might begin to dare to receive from God blessings on behalf of others, then to pass them on by faith. We do not have to be with the person in need to do this, in fact we can do it in their absence and without their knowing. Why not dare to do it? Stand before God and hold out your hands to him cupped to receive a blessing on behalf of your wife or husband, friend or relative, then pass it to them by faith: do it consistently, believing in his power and **watch them** being transformed. It is the most exciting thing you can do; see God's power working here on planet earth as you take up your area of authority and claim his blessing on it by faith. This is real. It is dealing with the God of heaven on the basis of revealed fact. And it works. Faith in action.

Another way in which we are called to exercise our priesthood is in praying for our nation. Firstly, we are to bring before our God the areas of national guilt accepting them as ours and pleading for forgiveness through the blood of Christ. Only thus may the terrible guilt of our society be cleansed – exploitation of third and fourth world countries, refusal to defend the weak and persecuted, the toll of innocent lives under our abortion laws, all the detritus of a selfish materialist society. If it is not to sink beneath the weight of its own guilt we must bear that guilt to Christ. That is our task.

Prayer is militant action
The Church of Christ is also called to be an army of priests who so surround heaven with prayer, that the whole body of Christ is touched by heavenly power in every part and constantly renewed. That should be our on-going state. Of course, there is a problem – Satan has no intention of allowing this to happen if he can possibly prevent it. He is mortally afraid of the Church because he knows better than we do the enormous extent of the authority vested in it by its Lord. For Revelation does not call us just priests, but **kings** and priests. And kings, in Old Testament thought, were not effete armchair critics of the world around, they

were warriors called to the frontiers of the kingdom to do battle with the encroaching enemy, turn him back and expand the area of God's people. We are called to be warrior kings. In New Testament times when the thought of royal authority was more clearly formulated kings were expected to reign – that is, to exhibit regal authority and control by the strength of their own character and kingdom.

The enemy strongholds in our country and the world will never be broken down until we come against them in prayer that is filled with the power of the 'Lord of Hosts', the God of battles. When we consciously do that we will at last be acting as kings and priests, and our nation will begin to feel the impact of our prayers. The entrenched powers of private and institutional greed, the vicious exploiters of the young and the inadequate, the anti-human purveyors of sexual perversion and indulgence; the merchants of pornography, the drug dealers, all who offer liberty and only lead their victims into greater bondage, who serve money and power subjecting others to tyranny. All these have their roots and hidden power in the spiritual power of Satan. If we want to attack such powers locally and nationally we must learn to act as warrior priests. We must hit the enemy where it hurts – in his power base. Prayer has rightly been called the Christian's ICBM (Inter-Cosmic Ballistic Missile) because it is not limited to any local area: not even to this world, galaxy or universe. Real prayer, specifically directed against the enemy himself will seek him, find him and hit him wherever in creation he tries to hide.

Prayer touches the world of suffering and pain
Just look around the world for a few moments. Consider what sin has done. That awful moment in Eden when Eve was promised insight, knowledge and freedom has resulted in blindness, ignorance and bondage for the whole human race. Tonight two thirds of the world will go to bed hungry and probably twenty thousand will die of starvation. Others

will endure another night of misery and pain as multiple sclerosis, muscular dystrophy, leukaemia, cancers, malaria, leprosy and countless other diseases and infections continue their grim and relentless cull of humanity. Think of the casualties of war – victims of Hiroshima and the scarred children of napalm attack and those suffering because of nuclear accidents. A world of torment and pain. The terrible private suffering of the mentally ill. Then those who have been brought under direct satanic tyranny – by involvement in ouija boards, spiritualism, black/white magic, TM, and so-called Divine Light as well as deliberate acts of rebellion against God. As Gandalf said in *Lord of the Rings*, 'I pity even his slaves!'

Think of this empire of misery and then say if your heart and mind do not revolt against the hellish author, and long to instal the rightful King again. No wonder David said, *'I hate God's enemies with a perfect hatred.'* There is the right direction for all our anger and hatred at suffering – against Satan and his hordes of demonic deceiving spirits.

> *'For our fight is not against any physical enemy: it is against organisations and powers that are spiritual. We are up against the unseen power that controls this dark world, and spiritual agents from the very headquarters of evil.'*[4]

So this is prayer – how can we think it is boring? In particular this is the purpose of corporate prayer: to stand together against all the power of hell and win.

> *'Therefore you must wear the whole armour of God that you may be able to resist evil in its day of power, and that even when you have fought to a standstill you may still stand your ground.'*[5]

Living as we do in a world that is in the hand of the enemy we must be prepared with the right equipment if we are to be able to resist his assaults. For attack us he will. He knows he must beat us or lose everything. He will attack our honesty, our morals, our stability and our peace of mind; constantly he will seek to undermine our trust in the goodness of God.

> *'Take your stand then with truth as your belt, righteousness your breastplate, the gospel of peace firmly on your feet, salvation as your helmet, and in your hand the sword of the Spirit, the Word of God. Above all, be sure you take faith as your shield, for it can quench every burning missile the enemy hurls at you.'*[6]

As well as the sword of the Spirit, Paul also commands the Ephesians to go on the offensive against the enemy with *'all prayer'*. God has given the world and its dominion into the hands of people and he needs people to yield it back to him before he can act in power in it. That is the purpose of the prayer *'Let your kingdom come.'* It commands the reign of God in that area of life over which we pray. This is the fourth function of our praying. Of course, its power depends on our faith and persistence and our agreement in prayer with the body of Christ.

Prayer grasps God's weapons
In praying against the powers of darkness we need to remember that we have been given certain very simple but effective weapons. These weapons derive their power not just from their history and certainly not from any mere magical power in the words themselves. They are effective against all the power of the enemy as they are used under the orders of the Holy Spirit. Any group praying against evil powers must commit themselves to the control of the Spirit of Christ. Only as he leads them will they see enemy strongholds destroyed. For the weapons of our warfare are mighty through God to destroy strongholds.

First among them is the **Bible** itself. As we quote this against Satan we do at least know it is utterly true and inspired. Mind you, he is not above using or misusing it himself to confuse us. He did it to Jesus in the wilderness.[7] But the Bible is a sword, so use it. Take its words and thrust them at the powers of darkness; they will feel them and shrink back.

Another weapon is the **blood** of Christ – the sign of his death and therefore of our forgiveness, it has great power to release people from satanic bondage. It is essential before any group of people sets out to pray against some local or national stronghold of the enemy that they do so as people who are consciously claiming the cleansing of the death of Jesus. Then there is the **cross** of Christ. Brought against the Devil it has two values – it is the place where, in Christ, I was crucified and died, thus passing out of the control of Satan, and it is the place of Satan's own total defeat. Because of the person who inflicted that defeat, the **name of Jesus** is also a great weapon. We must use that name conscious of its great authority. Paul declares that every knee must bow at the name of Jesus, because God has *'given the name above every name'*, his own name of 'Lord' to Jesus Christ. We must never forget to deploy the **Holy Spirit** around us by faith, so that the enemy always sees us covered with him, just like the wrestlers of ancient Greece who covered themselves in oil. It made them hard to get hold of, and almost impossible to pin down. The Holy Spirit gives Satan the same problem.

Prayer establishes God's rule
There is no point, of course, in our attacking and displacing enemy power unless at the same time, we establish afresh God's authority. This we do by speaking a command in faith through the Holy Spirit which begins to release the power of God's kingdom here in the earth. Jesus taught us to pray, *'Let your kingdom come, let your will be done on earth as it is in heaven.'* This instruction still calls us to speak out certain kinds of prayer with royal authority. For we are Children of the King called to reign with him. He wants our words to be full of regal power so that through us the goodness and majesty of God will speak into the sadness

and poverty of our planet. When we pray like this, we proclaim the kingdom of God here on earth before the return of Jesus Christ. All the power of God gets in behind such prayers. The voice may be weak and the words mere words, but holy reality pours into them to fill them with power and clothe them with authority. Our proclamation begins to establish the Kingdom which is to come. Surely our prayers should be gripped anew by a spirit of aggression and defiance against the enemy. Certainly we should thrill to the idea that through us a little part of this world can become the kingdom of our God and of his Christ.

Long before we attempt to do anything in this fallen world – whether feeding the hungry, lifting the oppressed or preaching the good news – we should first saturate the scene in authoritative prayer of the kind that says, 'By the authority of Jesus the Lord; we defy you Satan, you and all your servant powers. We shall not fear you. In this area we confront you with the blood and cross of Christ. Lord Jesus reign here, now. Father let your kingdom be released here. Let your will be done in this bit of our planet. Pour your spirit in here to fill it with your life.' When people pray like this, it is the most practical thing they can do.

A word of warning. We are talking about heavenly warfare. There is an enemy and he will do his best to fight back. So such prayer may be very costly. In any case no one should engage in prayer like this alone – at the very least this kind of spiritual offensive is the work of two or three people. By such prayer situations are changed, mountains are moved, people are blessed and God is glorified. Financially it is the best way to work because it establishes change at the roots before we attempt to bring in organisational or physical change. By such prayer, we establish spiritual change as we take command in the Spirit of God. Our destiny is to *'reign in life through the one man Jesus Christ'*. That is how we are meant to live. Not as beaten-up, hopeless failures but as warrior kings, heartening to our brothers and sisters, glorifying to God and terrifying to Satan.

Prayer is for you

This is **your** destiny; to learn to exercise the authority of God as his representative in the enemy-held territory of this world. For this the Creator himself fathered you, loved and chose you before the world was made or the stars were formed, that you might inherit a share in his kingdom to reign with him for ever. Only you can do this. There is an area of life which is uniquely yours; over it your authority is pre-eminent and for it you are primarily responsible. Exactly where it is will be revealed as you let the Holy Spirit lead you into deeper spiritual commitment in various areas of living. And do not dare to think that God would not entrust something to you; every human being has spiritual respons-ibility for a certain part of the world. Otherwise Jesus would have included in the parable of the talents not just servants with five, two and one talent, but also those with no talent.[8] The master had given **all** of them something for which they were then responsible to him. By the power vested in you as a child of the Kingdom pray the authority of God down into your area – only you can do it. Your family, your job, your corner of the world, no matter how small, no one else can do it. All of heaven is trembling on the rim of the world to see what you will do, the saints of the past are cheering you on, so 'boldly go' with all the power of God to extend his authority 'where no one has gone before'.

God has promised to go with you. He will.

> Lord, teach me to pray.
> In my best moments I long to spend hours with you.
> Then I find something else to do.
> Forgive me.
> Teach me to know what real prayer is.
> Let me enter into your heart.
> Teach me to pray.
> Amen.

In this book we have tried to look at the call of God as it comes to each of us, to bring us into God's eternal destiny.

In lovingly making a plan for you and me God had an ultimate purpose in mind – a purpose which goes far beyond the frontiers of space and time and out into eternity. In our next chapter we try to glimpse where that may take us.

Chapter 10

The Last Battle

'The whole fury and might of the enemy must very soon be turned on us. Hitler knows that he must break us in this island or lose the war. Let us therefore brace ourselves to our duties and so bear ourselves that if the British Empire and its Commonwealth last for a thousand years, men will still say "This was their finest hour."'[1]

The Kingdom of God will come

In June 1940 when Winston Churchill spoke these words, the armies of Adolph Hitler seemed invincible. Few people expected Britain to be able to resist them. Few outside of Britain would have given 'the British Empire and its Commonwealth' more than another year of existence. Yet filled with faith in 'Providence' and inspired by the trust of King George VI, Churchill could look at the possibility that it would last for a thousand years.

Now that Empire, like all the proud empires of the earth, has faded away. Adolph Hitler, George VI and Winston Churchill are all dead, fast receding into the history books. 'That's the way it is.' All human structures, political or physical; all leaders, good or evil, finally fade away and die. Yet they are not meaningless, they point to something else: an eternal reality. All who are in Christ are already participating in that reality.

Heralds of another King, Jesus: we serve a nobler empire

and inhabit a richer commonwealth than any empire of earth could ever be. Incapable of being measured in thousands or even millions of years, it is eternal – the kingdom of heaven. We are citizens of this new kingdom, members of its imperial family. A kingdom of love, it is not built like an earthly empire on the backs of helpless slaves. Instead it consists of one great family born into Christ, bearing his nature, so that glad service is the natural outcome of love.

The kingdom of darkness opposes
But as we saw earlier, this world lies in the hands of another ruler, the Prince of Darkness. Because of Christ's victory at Calvary he knows that he is defeated – he cannot win. Desperately he clings to a last vain hope. This earth is to be the place from which the final blow will be struck against him; so if he can prevent the chosen instrument, the Church, from mounting that assault ... All his energies therefore are directed against the Church. In his intricate scheming and deception there is one overriding strategy: defeat the Church; divide it, defile it, destroy it. The worldwide body of Christ is the island of God's kingdom on earth surrounded by the ocean of human societies dominated by materialism and greed, ethnic rivalries, demonic hatreds and religious pride. He knows he must break us in this island or lose the war, finally and irrevocably.

How long before he pours out the last reserves of his fury and might in the ultimate assault? Jesus sat on the Mount of Olives looking at the Temple. The disciples asked him about the end of the world. He told them that in the last period of history, before his coming as Lord to wind up the affairs of earth, there would be a final and most terrible attack on the Church all over the world. This co-ordinated wave of persecution seems to be preceded by a period of increasing unrest in the world: ethnic wars, conflict between nations and natural disasters. It seems that competing international alliances will unite in hatred of the Church and of Israel. Now such periods have occurred before. People have, in the past, identified Napoleon,

Mussolini and Hitler among others, as the prime mover of Satan's power, the Antichrist. But is is worth looking carefully at our own era of history. After all, the return of Jesus Christ will not always be in the future. For one generation it will cease to be a future promise and become an instantly present reality. Maybe our own generation will be the one to see it happen!

Our culture is collapsing
If we look at the evidence in my own nation and in western society as a whole we do see certain tendencies which if they continue will bring about the collapse of the western democracies. That clear-eyed prophet Solzhenityn, after his release from what was then the Soviet Union, was briefly the darling of the Western press. Then it was realized that he had not emerged from persecution in order to give his seal of approval to our capitalist society, or our liberal morality. In fact he thundered his disapproval. The liberal establishment who would rather live in dreams mocked his warnings. But they are terrifyingly real, It is a fact that no society can survive if all its pillars – religion, the family, law, government and work – are destroyed at the same time. In my country and many others this process is going on at the moment – all those pillars have become frighteningly eroded and undermined. The lessons of history are clear and inevitable – if this goes on, collapse into chaos or a violent and bloody revolution is assured. The eventual outcome of such a collapse would be government by force, a totalitarian state whether of the left or the right which would certainly put the church under dreadful pressure.

Now this is not the worst thing that could happen. Down the centuries the vast majority of real Christians have lived under pressure or direct persecution. Even today the greater part of the body of Christ is living under threat. And because churches in that situation quickly learn what is really important, they are often healthier than the churches of the 'free' world.

In spite of this, I believe we are called to pray that the Lord will act in power in our nations and in western society to save us from deserved destruction; because although persecution produces a healthy Church, it hurts the weak – the young and the very old, and those wounded by life. May the loving God have mercy on us and give to the Church a true change of heart so that through her a great river of life may be poured into the community, and thus our whole society be changed. It can happen – powerful prayer and authoritative preaching have changed the course of history before: they can again.

The nations are in turmoil
The world as a whole is increasingly troubled. When the Berlin Wall was demolished in late 1989 it was seen by many as ushering in a new age. Over the few months before and after that event the other nations of the Soviet Union ousted their old-style communist governments. The Soviet Union itself in spite of its final withdrawal from Afghanistan still seemed inviolable. But within two years the unthinkable had happened: the Union of Soviet Socialist Republics had disintegrated. It was a moment of supreme triumph for the Western democracies, which had been locked in Cold War, with what one US President had called 'the Evil Empire'. Writing just a few years after these events it seems like a lost world – there is security of a sort, in knowing you have an obvious identifiable enemy.

Now that the monolithic 'Soviet bloc' has gone down to history, far older hatreds are emerging. Tribal hatred and ethnic rivalries are plunging large sections of the previous Soviet empire into chaos, violence and war. It is as if a great concrete gravestone has been smashed and the old demons are emerging from the tainted earth. Far from heralding a new world order, the collapse of the Eastern bloc has left us in a much more unstable and dangerous world: a time of increasing uncertainty and of growing anxiety. The most powerful idea emerging in many of these countries, including Russia, is the system that was apparently destroyed in the last days of the Second World War – Fascism. The Nazis are back on the streets of the cities of Europe. National Socialism whatever its national identity, is powerfully attractive to powerless and frightened people.

Consequently violence between national and tribal groupings is increasing – in Europe, Asia, India and Africa, while racial tensions threaten to tear apart the US. Seeking to combat all this, fundamentalist liberals are becoming increasingly intolerant as they seek to impose 'political correctness' in every area of life. When they emerge on to the streets to fight racism, they are at least as violent as the fascists they hate. They have become the mirror image of the Nazis they oppose. It is the curse of our fallenness. When we seek to do our best we are often at our worst. It seems hopeless. How should we respond?

Jesus said,

> *'On the earth nations will be in anguish and perplexity at the roaring and tossing of the sea. Men will faint from terror, apprehensive of what is coming on the world, for the heavenly bodies will be shaken ... When these things begin to take place, stand up and lift up your heads because your redemption is drawing near.'*[2]

Violence fills the earth

Violence within nations is a worldwide problem – it reflects the lessening influence of the specifically Christian idea that every individual is valuable. This process is very noticeable in post-Christian societies like Britain and the United States. August 2, 1993 edition of *Time* magazine chronicled what it called 'the deadly love affair between America's youth and firearms'. The article spoke of 'the inexplicable despair that torments so many American teenagers' declaring 'some days, guns are just a defence against boredom that comes from a lack of guidance and direction'.

In Europe the same boredom is all too evident with the same resort to violence. In Germany gangs of youths roam the streets festooned with swastikas, looking for foreign workers to beat up, or even burn to death in their homes. The great majority of Germans and the government seem impotent to stop them. Here in England, drug barons battle for control: gun battles in the streets, once unthinkable, are regular occurrences in some inner city areas. In Russia gang members sport Kalashnikov rifles that once belonged to the Red Army, while weapons grade plutonium can be bought for a quarter of a million dollars. We do not have the time to look at these situations in any detail or at the rest of the world.

People are beyond restraint
The teenagers of the nineties have inherited the poisoned legacy of the flower children of the sixties and seventies. 'Make love not war', was the cry then, as if these two things were diametrically opposed. But the philosophy: 'If it feels good, do it', meant that people opened the door to the tyranny of their own sexual desires. Sex as sport, the search for pleasure, the worship of physical sensation, devalued the ideas of relationship and emotional commitment.

The lessening of restraints in the atmosphere of 'the new morality' led only to people becoming more deeply enslaved by the old immorality. In their pain and guilt they lashed out at the rules of moral conduct as instruments of oppression. Any suggestion of sexual self-control was greeted by the cry of 'Repression'! The atmosphere of indulgence was compounded by the increasing affluence of the Western world. Built as this was on the economic oppression of the Third and Fourth World it would only make things worse. We were living in a luxury we had not earned by the equivalent amount of hard work. If we believe in God we must believe in accountability. Only a fool would deny that judgement hangs over us like the sword of Damocles, suspended by a thread of mercy.

Maybe this generation of young people is part of our judgement. We brought them up to expect instant gratification and they have learned well. Often watched over more by a television screen than a parent, they have a constant need for sensation, for visual stimulation. Denied the opportunity for real struggle they never know the satisfaction of real achievement. Full of bubbling energy, untrained in its constructive expression, they release it in aggression and violence. Geared to sitting, staring passively at a screen, receiving sometimes the most horrifying images, their sensitivities to death and suffering are dulled. Frequently demanding instant solutions to complex problems they are the spoilt grandchildren of consumerism. Empty, frustrated and angry, they are easy prey for the drug pushers. We have given them everything except what they really need, inner meaning, a focus other than themselves, a reason to live, faith in the eternal God.

Sexual corruption spreads

Meanwhile in our unrestrained hedonism, our obedience to the 'anything goes' sexual ethic, we have opened the way for them to become victims of the most perverted fantasies, while they are still children. We have failed to acknowledge that one man's 'freedom of expression' may become another's oppression. Some academics even try to provide an apologetic for paedophiles declaring that 'they really care' for their victims. I will not deny that even a child molester can have human feelings. But it is difficult to believe that humanity has anything to do with the way that children of five or six years old are sexually used dozens of times a day in the sex markets of Bangkok (usually by European, American and Japanese men). The pornography industry – one of the fastest growing sections of the Western economy – provides a constant stream of filth to stimulate these men, not to mention videos and computer material that glorify bondage, sado-masochism and rape. Such material degrades women while building up hatred of the female in the men who watch. It encourages rapists and sex murderers as it did Peter Sutcliffe, the 'Yorkshire Ripper'. Yet the liberal establishment in the world of the arts and media is, by and large, more concerned with defending freedom of expression than condemning this exploitative muck. So violence and sexual corruption continue to grow in our Western society while the music plays ever louder and angrier.

Islam is advancing

Here in Britain some observers are beginning to look at the relative decency of life in Islamic countries. Some of the finest representatives of that way of life live here. We see their commitment to prayer, the stability of their family life and feel a tinge of envy. With the collapse of international communism, Islam is increasingly claiming the moral high ground as the best alternative to the moral corruption of the Western world, which Muslims regard as the Christian world. Yet its record with regard to the treatment of women is nothing to boast about. And violence is enshrined at the heart of its teaching and development.

It is undeniably true that Christendom's history is full of gratuitous violence, often justified by religious slogans – for example the crusades – but such violence is actually contrary to the teaching of Jesus himself, more proof that there is no such thing as a 'Christian nation'. The vital difference is the sanctifying of violence in Islam, its endorsement by Muhammed as a method of advancing the faith. In the world at the end of the twentieth century the recent great resurgence of Islam seems likely to continue, fuelled by a new self-respect in the Islamic nations. For the vast oil riches of the Arabs and their restored sense of power together with the moral weakness of the western nations and the disasters of rampant technology have given them a new confidence in their own culture and heritage.

Though all Islamic nations are theoretically part of one body, Dar al Islam, only one issue truly unites them: hatred of the state of Israel. The Gulf War did shake that unity for a while, but Israel's subsequent actions have restored it. There is broad agreement on another issue – they all oppose the church of Jesus Christ. Now, of course, the way this works out varies greatly in different nations. But it is worth remembering that many Muslim clergy and teachers assert it is impossible to be a proper Muslim unless the whole of society is governed by Islamic principles based on the Koran. Islam is a power-system aimed at total control of national life. Within such control there is no room for individual decisions on important issues like religion. Evangelism, therefore, is anathema to Islamic nations. Christians are committed to evangelism.

Israel at the centre of events

Let us think again about Israel. From the beginning the Church has affirmed that Jesus is the Alpha and Omega, the A and Z, the beginning and the end. Through Him all things were made. Through Him all things will be brought to final fulfilment. In Him was creation. In Him will be consummation. So it has always been part of orthodox faith to affirm that Jesus Christ 'will come again'. Some people have turned his expression into a poetical one, or perhaps so spiritualised it that it no longer means what it says. But its plain meaning remains, the meaning that Jesus himself gave it. He, the eternal son of God made flesh, will return to this earth from his place of authority in the heavenlies. He will come with supernatural power and glory so great that he will be instantly recognisable to the church and the world. He will come when the world is in an hour of great torment to take control, and usher in the kingdom of God on earth.

There are many schools of teaching about this event and I do not intend to try to pick my way through that minefield in this chapter! Enough to say that most systems agree on one thing: the return of Jesus Christ is somehow tied up with the rebirth of Israel. This is because Jesus himself made a clear link between the two when he said that Jerusalem would be 'trodden down' by the non-Jewish peoples until the times of the non-Jewish peoples **were at an end**.[3] The founding of Israel in 1948 is therefore vitally important – even more significant, however, is the date 1967. For this was the year of the Six-Day War when Israel took back Jerusalem – in the words of Israeli leaders 'for ever'.

It seems obvious that the day the Israelis took over the Old City of Jerusalem the plans of God moved into a new phase.

As to Israel's own position in the world, this is likely to become more and more isolated. We saw occasions when the Communist and Islamic blocs united against Israel. The western nations have all modified their attitude of support for her because of the oil weapon held by the Islamic countries in North Africa, Arabia and the Middle East. Israel appears to be the eye of a huge storm centre. Sometimes the storm boils and rages, sometimes it calms. One day it could engulf the whole world.

The Church under threat

It is clear that the 'coming of the Lord' is tied up with a certain pattern of events. And it is not difficult to see the possibility of that pattern emerging as we look at the current world scene. It may be that at last the travail of the earth is finally about to bring forth the second coming of the Lord. In any coming to birth there are often false alarms and 'false labours' and these can produce a feeling that 'the baby will never come'. But it does. Just because there have been other moments in the history of the Church when people felt the return was imminent and were disappointed this does not mean that he is not on the way. We must consider these things soberly and with open mind avoiding both hysteria and cynicism.

It may be that we will see what the Church has longed for; the veil hiding heaven from earth torn apart to allow the Prince on his white horse to ride through, bring down the forces of the enemy and at last take the Church, his bride, to be with himself. If we really are on the brink of this great event then almost certainly the Church is going to enter the hour of its deepest trial, its most terrible suffering: the time of universal persecution.

It may seem improbable that such persecution could arise in an easy going society in which 'tolerance' is the greatest virtue. Yet there is the very issue that may trigger our pain.

Christians are bound to honour all people, respecting their right to believe as they choose, and acknowledging whatever there may be of truth in other religions. But we are committed to Jesus Christ as the Truth. Where other religions differ from Jesus we have to say, respectfully and humbly, that they are wrong. Jesus Christ is the Way the Truth and the Life. Even though people may come to know the living God outside of the Christian revelation, like Abraham did, or worship outside it like Naaman did, they can only come to the Father through Jesus. This forces people to decide for him or against him. It makes them feel uncomfortable. The truth remains. He is not just a localised deity. He is Lord of all. It is not difficult to see that in some circumstances, such an affirmation no matter how courteous its expression, would offend those whose only absolute truth is that there is no absolute truth. Persecution could come to us.

What are we to do then?

God is still in control

First, recognise that God makes no mistakes. If such a time of pressure is coming and you are to live through it, this is because he has chosen you to stand for him at such a time. It is a privilege. Remember that this last moment of pain for the Church will be its 'finest hour'. One of the great honours of eternity will be this one – to have stood for Jesus Christ in the 'finest hour' of the Church; the Bible makes it clear that such people bear special glory. So if it comes in our time, be glad! Because that is what Jesus said:

> 'Happy are those who are persecuted because they do what God requires; the kingdom of heaven belongs to them!
> Happy are you when people insult you and persecute you and tell all kinds of evil lies against you because you are my followers.
> Be happy and glad, for a great reward is kept for you in heaven.'[4]

147

Understand that in such a situation God has chosen you, the special unique individual that you are, to represent him, as his child: so that in the midst of cruelty and pain the world will know that there is a loving Father and creator, and that Jesus Christ is truly the one sent by him. This is your privilege and destiny at all times. So do be glad!

Be glad anyway. Even if the Lord's coming is yet delayed for a thousand years you will have the unrepeatable privilege of being you. Live that out gladly day by day. Live originally, not as a boring stereotype, a copy of all the other 'standard' Christians. We are not modules, but children. God the Father rejoices in our individuality for it glorifies him. That is why he made us. Jesus Christ was the most original person the world has ever known. He was himself. And you are called to be like him. That is, you are called so to live under the loving guidance of the Father that you become truly yourself. So take the standards, the commands and the promises of the Word of God; make them your own and go out into all the world to live as nobody ever lived before.

O Lord,
You know I have no desire to be persecuted or to live in great tribulation. But when hard times come, I will trust you. You will carry me through.
You will bring me through the darkness, pain and suffering into the joy of your kingdom. I will come into your great Light and live with you forever. Therefore give me grace to obey you always.
Through Jesus who suffered and entered glory.
Amen.

Chapter 11

Where No Man Has Gone Before

'What is heaven to me, Lord?
Surely it is nothing other than Jesus my God
For if heaven is that which is above all things
Then, Lord God, you alone are heaven to my soul.'

Walter Hilton, *Ladder of Perfection*[1]

Heaven waits for us

We are on the greatest journey possible, a voyage far
beyond the bounds of our wildest imagining. We are on our
way into the heart of God. And he has declared his intention to unveil to us the endless mysteries, not only of
creation but of heaven; the realm of his reality, the unending vistas of his glory. Beyond the dark doorway of death,
eternity stretches like a vast unexplored country full of
adventures waiting to be lived.

One further word about death. We may naturally dread
the process of dying; the sudden shock of accident, the
descent into pain of a cancer, the long dissolution of degen-
erative disease. But Hebrews tells us that Jesus, 'suffered
death so that by the grace of God he might taste death for
everyone.'[2] Whatever death awaits us, Jesus has in the
mysterious agony of the cross, already tasted it for us. He
waits in the doorway to be our companion through it, to
bring us into the entrance to the celestial city.

In the church today we seem to have suffered a loss of
nerve about heaven. We do not speak of it with the glad

certainty Jesus gives us. Perhaps we have been too mes-
merised by the unfolding discovery of the greatness of the
creation around us. One thing is sure, heaven is greater and
more glorious than anything we have discovered or have
yet to discover in the material universe. We need this
certainty if we are to be free to live in this world as we
should. For there is a great deal to be done.

We are children of the eternal family

There is a world to be won to the love of Christ. The Father
and Maker yearns over the suffering of the earth and longs
to wrap the wounded millions in his arms of love. And that
is why you are firstly to be his child. God did not create
human doings, but human beings. The most important
thing about you is not your function out in the world or
inside the church, but who you are in God. As you grow in
that identity, you will increasingly be able to relate to
others in Christ. Joined to each other we discover the
power of the body of Christ. Together we can accomplish
what we could never do alone. United we find there is more
power for service, inspiration in worship and mutual protection in the spiritual war. Then in relationship with him
and each other we are able, from the security of family
relationship, to go into all the world, with the love and
good news of Jesus.

Look at these marvellous words from Revelation:

> *'And they have conquered him by the blood of the
> Lamb and by the word of their testimony, for they loved
> not their lives even unto death.'*[3]

That is your destiny: to conquer the enemy. But not
alone! Twice in this verse the word 'they' is used. The
defeat of Satan is something that is only accomplished
corporately. We need each other. But the actions men-
tioned are things that must be done individually. So the
defeat of Satan can only come when Christians band
together to stand individually against him. Your private

victory will benefit your brother. My lonely defeat will weaken my sister. We stand as precious individuals joined in united action – a single body with many members: the body of Christ.

We are members together of one Church

Just as we need each other as individuals we need each other in our denominations and streams. No denomination in the church has a complete understanding or a perfect expression of God's revelation. Each denomination fills a gap in the understanding of others. The Anglicans need the House Churches, the Brethren need the Pentecostals, the Catholics need the Baptists. Even within denominations there are differing views of biblical truth. Looking at the Gospels it is perfectly possible to construct an Evangelical Jesus, a Liberal Christ, a Catholic Son of Man, or a Charismatic Son of God. The elements for those portraits are all there. Most of us can cope with one, two or even three of them. Four stretches us too far. The glorious problem with Jesus is that he is always greater than our conceptions of him. He is impossible to contain. He is the living Lord. Only together as the whole Body of Christ united across the centuries and throughout the world will we ever be able to show forth his fullness.

We are soldiers called to victory

In the meantime we each have a part to play. Your destiny as an individual is to conquer the enemy: firstly by a continual attitude of repentance that allows God to cleanse you through the death of Christ. As God's sacrificial lamb he took the blame for you and me and carried all our guilt. His blood, the sign of that death for us, is our weapon of defence whenever we are attacked by guilt or fear. I am forgiven. You are forgiven. The blood is the sign and guarantee of that forgiveness.

Secondly, your destiny is to conquer by your testimony; your own witness to Jesus Christ. No one else can know him as you do and so no one else can talk about him as you can. This is your testimony: what Jesus Christ has done for you and what he has become to you. Satan fears that kind of story because the proclamation of your life in the kingdom of Jesus Christ, is to him the proclamation of his doom.

Thirdly, these weapons gain their power to overcome Satan by the commitment of your own life. We are not just talking about a message of words. We are talking about a new life lived under the authority and command of Jesus Christ the Lord.

The words, *'they loved not their lives even unto death,'* indicate the total commitment necessary to defeat Satan. These people in John's vision were prepared to die for the sake of Jesus. Their lives, important to them as they were, were committed totally to Christ. He mattered more than life.

When King Jesus reigns there is no room for any other monarch – not even you! Often we sing 'He is Lord, He is Lord' and we do not realise how dangerous it is. For to sing it without meaning it, is to invite the Lord of whom we sing to come to us and assess just how great that Lordship is. Judgement begins at the house of God – for God is determined to get his family right and happy before him. So apply yourself to discipline. Determine to live obediently to the Father God whatever he may ask. Live courageously, as if your life does not matter compared to God's kingdom. Whatever happens – boldly go!

Jesus has promised,

> *'Happy are those whose greatest desire is to do what God requires; God will satisfy them fully.'*[4]

We worship a great God

And that is a good point to stop and consider the ultimate aim of all that we have looked at. *'God will satisfy them fully'* because he is the great God. And the greatness of God is something that seems to be missing from our consciousness so much of the time. We know it in theory but have not truly been gripped by it as a reality.

There are two words that taken together serve as a starting point for the greatness of God. These two words are missing from most modern Christianity. Their omission from our understanding is responsible for much of our spiritual poverty.

Majesty and mystery.

Majesty. God is the great King. He is monarch of all universes in all dimensions.

What we know of this universe beggars description. There is no way we can begin to encompass it in our minds. Our earth is one of nine planets circling the Sun which is one of over a hundred billion stars in our home galaxy, the Milky Way. The Milky Way is a fairly standard galaxy, some are much larger, others much smaller. Travelling at the speed of light (300,000 kilometres per hour) it would take 100,000 years to cross it. To get to the furthest edge of the universe itself would take 200,000 times that – an unimaginable 20,000,000,000 years at the speed of light. Almost all the stars we can see in the sky are in our home galaxy, the Milky Way. Some 'stars' are actually distant galaxies. In this universe there are uncounted hundreds of billions of galaxies, each one an enormous starsystem in its own right. He reigns over them all – the Lord in majesty. And this aspect of his character is like a great, wide, deep river flowing fullflood, irrestible in its course. To be aware of it is to be bathed in a great calm, the stillness of eternity. You are in the presence of an immense and unimaginable strength. He is God of all gods, King of all kings, maker of all things. The everlasting Father, the Bible calls him. Vaster than we ever imagined, his majesty rests not in the physical splendour of his creation, but in eternity.

We reverence a holy God

The total purity of his character is revealed in the blinding light of holiness, the white heat of selfless love and the absolute moral integrity of his person. He is the same. From eternity to eternity he is God. He is always all these things without effort or conflict. He is always being what he is being. His life which is total, absolute, full and rich, constantly radiates from every part of his being a joy so complete, so immeasurable that one touch of it would be enough to unmake us. He is great. His grandeur and magnificence tower above us like mountains taller than we can ever know and still his voice calls us on into himself.

Consider, too, the greatness that from the immense shining peaks of his eternal holiness could descend to be a human! An ordinary man in a world dirty with selfishness, pride, greed and lust. And he did not just touch these things in passing – he sank to the very bottom of the pits of hell to plumb the deepest depravity of the worst man. We will never know the mystery behind the words *'he was made sin for us'* – he suffered more in hell than any person ever before or since. He was himself undefiled yet he soaked up the defilement and absorbed the punishment of every man and woman. God be praised! The greater we see his holiness to be, the greater we know his love is. He came down from the height of his holiness and joy in the darkest pit of guilt. His love is greater, always greater. And his love is part of the mystery.

We seek a God beyond us
Mystery. The God who is never static though always at rest. Always becoming yet also unchanging. And the greater he is, the greater the mystery he presents. Always higher, wider, deeper than we have yet discovered; he is always revealing to us more of the mystery of his being. The one who is 'being what he is being and becoming what he is becoming' has made us uniquely what we are so that we can uncover some hidden pathway of his character that no one else could ever find.

The real quest is here – as God eternally unfolds his being, he invites you into himself on a vast journey of exploration which will never exhaust the subject. Always there is more. *'Great is the Lord,'* says the psalmist, *'and greatly to be praised, his greatness is unsearchable.'* That is our glorious, mind-blowing task: to search out the

unsearchable greatness of God; to know the love of Christ
which goes way beyond our knowing and to explore the
richness of his person which is limitless and inexhaustible.
Oh, how great is our God! It is just as well we have eternity
– we are going to need it – and some more!

We begin this search here and now, and the pull of his
love draws us onward 'further in and higher up' as C.S.
Lewis says. Death becomes irrelevant, except that it
removes from us the hindrance of a fallen world and a
rather rebellious body of flesh. It takes away the veil that
hides the reality of heavenly things and makes them our
current possession for ever. But it also removes from us all
further opportunity of growing in Christ here in the earth,
and thus bringing glory and joy to him. Use your life wisely.
It matters what you do because the quest that begins in
faltering fashion here, in this fallen earth, goes on to find its
destiny in eternity. This is your God-given privilege and
eternal joy; to go on and on into the heart of God, to know
him and reveal him as he was never revealed before, and
the way you go is a way planned for you alone. This is what
the Bible means when it says that *we impart a secret and
hidden wisdom of God, which God decreed before the ages
"for our glorification."*[5] As we uncover layer upon layer of
his glory we ourselves will be transformed from one degree
of glory to another.

We serve a God who has promised us the Kingdom
If we look at the promises given by the Lord to the seven
churches in Revelation,[6] we can see the unfolding of his
destiny for humanity. These are conditional promises given
to those who overcome the temptations and pressures of
the world around, their fallen human nature and the Devil
himself. Of course, no one lives always in such a state. But
to the extent that we allow God to reign in these areas we
will enter these blessings.

(a)   *'To him who overcomes I will give the right to eat from
the tree of life which is in the paradise of God.'*

This first promise reverses the effect of the Fall. It gives to those who overcome, who repent and return to passionate love for God, the right to eat from heaven's tree of life and to live forever filled with the life of God.

(b) *'He who overcomes will not be hurt at all by the second death.'*

These people have lost everything for the sake of Christ, suffering, poor and persecuted, they have nothing to lose. When all that is not of God is burned up, they will suffer no pain. They are utterly free. May we be so.

(c) *'To him who overcomes I will give some of the hidden manna. I will also give him a white stone with a new name written on it known only to him who receives it.'*

Some live in places where there is much occult activity and rampant immorality. If they are faithful, Jesus promises he will mysteriously sustain and feed them with heavenly food, and he will also give them a new identity, an inner assurance that, 'I am who I should be. I belong.'

(d) *'To him who overcomes and does my will to the end, I will give authority over the nations –*

    He will rule them with an iron sceptre
    he will dash them to pieces like pottery –
    just as I have received authority from my Father.
    I will also give him the morning star.'

Corruption in the Church can only be overcome by total commitment to the will of God. To such people are promised two blessings; authority from Jesus comparable to that which he received from his Father, and the power to shine out in the darkest moment – the hour before the dawn.

(e) *'He who overcomes will like them be dressed in white. I will never blot out his name from the book of life, but will acknowledge his name before my Father and his angels.'*

Churches may have all the trappings of life but still be dead. If we do the works he has commanded, touching the hurting world with his compassion, refusing to compromise with immorality, he will clothe us in white and parade us before all heaven – imagine being led out before all those angels!

(f) *'Him who overcomes I will make a pillar in the temple of my God. Never again will he leave it. I will write on him the name of my God and the name of the city of God the new Jerusalem which is coming down out of heaven from my God and I will also write on him my own new name.'*

If we dare to witness for Jesus even when we are weak and afraid; he will make us an essential part of heaven, building us in like pillars. He will reveal through us the nature of God, the eternal destiny of the Church and the new revelation of Christ himself.

(g) *'To him who overcomes I will give the right to sit with me on my throne, just as I overcame and sat down with my Father on his throne.'*

When a church is affluent and feels full of spiritual blessings God often gets frozen out. But if we open up to him, let him share his life with us, and go with him to the cross, we shall overcome. He will lift us up to his throne to sit with him and reign with him.

So there is a pattern of blessing in these promises which starts with eternal life, progresses through the pledge of a new identity, into Christ-like authority over events in the nations, glorification before the angels, a new revelation of Christ himself and finally comes to sit on the throne of the Lord Jesus!

We shall reign with him

Nobody but God could ever have conceived such a daring plan – that we should share his throne and reign with him over the universe for ever and ever. And before you accuse me of megalomania just look at Revelation 22:4–5:

> *'They shall see his face, and his name shall be on their foreheads. And night shall be no more; they need no light of lamp or sun, for the Lord God will be their light, and **they shall reign for ever and ever.**'*

Where do we go from there? ... the answer is 'Where no one has ever gone.'

As we see him we shall be like him: because he reigns we shall share his sovereignty for ever. And this does not lessen his glory – it increases it. He is glorified in his children. So here is the meaning of all the pain and hardship, all the cost and difficulty of the Christian life. *'I consider that the sufferings of this present time are not worth comparing with the glory that is to be revealed to us.'*[7] Our pain in time is tied up with glory in eternity.

A new universe, a new earth where there never will be evil or suffering or pain any more, is what we are promised! As C.S. Lewis put it in *The Last Battle*: 'we then begin the real story, of which all that happened before was only the prologue and title page.' That is where it all starts.

God made you for himself, made you because, having fathered you in eternity before the world was made or the universe exploded into being from the Word, he loved you. He loves you still. Into the centre of his loving, into his heart, he has called you. No one else will do. You must go. Though you are completely superfluous – he has made you absolutely necessary. Necessary to himself, to his angels, to the Church, and even to me.

So go, go on into his heart.

Boldly go, knowing that the Maker awaits you in all the richness of his eternal fatherhood. Knowing too that the Son waits to show you the marks of his love for you so that your heart may exult with love for him. Knowing that the Spirit of God will be your constant companion for ever, filling you with the wild freedom of his holy life. Knowing that the mystery of your being was something treasured in the trinity from eternity and now the secret is to be shared with you. Knowing that you have been called to boldly go where no one has gone before.

God bless you.

Notes

Chapter 1

1. 1 Corinthians 15:19
2. Revelation 12:9–11 JBP
3. Micah 6:8 JBP
4. Psalm 18:19; 37:23

Chapter 2

1. 2 Timothy 4:7–8
2. Luke 2:49 GNB
3. Luke 4:18–19
4. Luke 4:43
5. John 8:28–9
6. John 5:19
7. Mark 10:45
8. John 12:27; 13:1
9. John 13:3
10. John 18:4
11. John 19:28

Chapter 3

1. Judges 16:28
2. 1 Corinthians 3:12–15

Chapter 4

1. Winston Churchill, Mansion House, 10 November, 1942
2. Genesis 1:26
3. Genesis 1:27
4. Genesis 2:24–25
5. Genesis 3:15
6. Luke 1:35
7. John 10:34–35

Chapter 5

1. Matthew 3:11; Mark 1:8; Luke 3:16; John 1:33
2. Acts 1:5
3. 1 Corinthians 12:13
4. Acts 11:16
5. Acts 2:32–33
6. Luke 11:13
7. 2 Corinthians 3:17

Chapter 6

1. Ephesians 1:4; Colossians 1:22
2. 1 Peter 2:9 GNB
3. Galatians 5:6
4. *Billy Bray, the King's Son*, Epworth Press
5. 1 Corinthians 14:26
6. 1 Corinthians 14:40

Chapter 7

1. 2 Kings 7:9 GNB
2. Mark 8:35; 10:29 AV
3. Mark 8:38; Luke 9:26
4. Mark 16:15
5. Romans 10:9–10
6. 1 Timothy 2:1–4
7. Psalm 136:1 NRSV
8. Galatians 5:24
9. Exodus 3:5–6 GNB
10. Deuteronomy 34:10

Chapter 8

1 Winston Churchill, *History of the Second World War*, Vol. 1. Writing of 10 May, 1940, when the King asked him to form a government.
2 See Aldous Huxley, *Ends and Means*, p. 270
3 Steve Turner, *A Way with Words*, Razor Books, 1979
4 John 5:39–40
5 Jeremiah 4:19
6 2 Timothy 2:15
7 Matthew 22:29 GNB

Chapter 9

1 Revelation 12:7–9
2 Exodus 17:8–16
3 Exodus 3:5
4 Ephesians 6:12 JBP
5 Ephesians 6:13 JBP
6 Ephesians 6:14–17 JBP
7 Luke 4:9–11
8 Matthew 25:14–30

Chapter 10

1 Winston Churchill, 18 June 1940
2 Luke 21:25–26; 28 NIV
3 Luke 21:24
4 Matthew 5:10–11 GNB

Chapter 11

1 Quoted in, *Praying with The English Mystics*, Triangle Books, 1990
2 Hebrews 2:9
3 Revelation 12:11
4 Matthew 5:6 GNB
5 1 Corinthians 2:7
6a Revelation 2:7
6b Revelation 2:11b
6c Revelation 2:17
6d Revelation 2:26–28
6e Revelation 3:5
6f Revelation 3:12
6g Revelation 3:21
7 Romans 8:18